PROFILES OF LEADERSHIP IN EDUCATION

Mark F. Goldberg

Phi Delta Kappa Educational Foundation
Bloomington, Indiana U.S.A.

Cover design by
Victoria Voelker

Phi Delta Kappa Educational Foundation
408 North Union Street
Post Office Box 789
Bloomington, Indiana 47402-0789
U.S.A.

Printed in the United States of America

Library of Congress Catalog Card Number 00-101820
ISBN 0-87367-826-5
Copyright © 2000 by Mark F. Goldberg

Whenever I do an interview, I think of all the small children not yet in school who are relying on us to provide them with a fine education, but most of all I think of my two preschool grandchildren, Maya Sivan and Gabriela Adi, who mean all the world to me and who represent all the children to me.

Table of Contents

Introduction 1

Madeline Hunter 7

Seymour Papert 15

Reuven Feuerstein 23

Shirley Brice Heath 33

Albert Shanker 41

Ernest Boyer 51

Rudolph Giuliani 59

Theodore Sizer 69

Stephen Jay Gould 79

James P. Comer 87

E.D. Hirsch Jr. 95

Claudio Sanchez 105

Mark Gearan 115

Shirley Strum Kenny 123

Dorothy Rich 133

Manuel Justiz 143

Hugh Price 153

Carol Gilligan 163

John I. Goodlad 173

About the Author 185

Introduction

The interviews collected in this book began with a proposal I made to Ronald Brandt, managing editor of *Educational Leadership*, in 1988. I told Ron that while I valued and benefited from many of the articles in his and other organizations' journals, I felt there was a serious lack of attention to the human face of educators who were having a considerable impact on the profession. Ron reminded me that *Educational Leadership* occasionally published interviews with well-known figures. But I wanted to write something different from those interviews.

I wanted to ask people such questions as who they were, how they came to be in education, who their heroes were, how they got started in their work, how their work had gotten through obstacles, what their dreams were in education, and what they felt was their career achievement.

Between 1989 and 1994, I interviewed 19 educators for *Educational Leadership*. Then, in 1994, I proposed a similar series to Pauline Gough at the *Phi Delta Kappan*. However, I wanted these new interviews to also include influential people who had a serious interest in education but who were not professional educators. Pauline accepted that proposal with the sensible proviso that the articles had to focus quite sharply on important education issues because that's what interests the *Kappan*'s readers. Since 1994, I have written about 20 interviews for the *Kappan*.

In reviewing the interviews I have done for both *Educational Leadership* and the *Kappan*, three things strike me. First, these interviews reflect a significant part of the national conversation about education since 1989. Of course, during 40 interviews with important educators and public figures with a deep and abiding interest in education, there will be common observations on school reform, school renewal, poverty, racism, technology, academic standards, assessment, and so many other education issues of our time. But in many ways these interviews were like a "conversation" across time and space. Interviewees often seemed to be engaged in a dialogue with someone I interviewed six months or two years earlier.

For example, I interviewed Stephen Jay Gould in New York City in January 1997. He observed that even the very extraordinary students he works with at Harvard "have no shared culture. There really isn't any centerpiece of knowledge you can assume people to have. Even a generation ago, you could assume that the most common Shakespearean and biblical quotations would be recognized by most students – but you just can't anymore." Eight months later in Charlottesville, Virginia, E.D. Hirsch Jr. emphasized the absence of a core curriculum in American schools: "I assumed there was a curriculum in the schools. What you find out is that this is a myth. Kids in the same building in the second grade are learning very different things from kids in another second grade in the same building."

This impression of extended conversations arose again and again. Claudio Sanchez, James Comer, and Shirley Brice Heath, for instance, all made similar statements about the effects of poverty and racism on disadvantaged children. Rudy Giuliani and Stephen Jay Gould, very different people, each used similar words and phrases ("standard," "gold standard," "template") and chose a model outside education to explain what they meant by education excellence: Giuliani cited the current work of the New York City Police Department, and Gould cited the baseball career of Joe DiMaggio.

Second, the people I interviewed were strikingly familiar with all of the details of their work, however complex or however many years it covered, almost never needing to pause to look something up but able to recall issues, dates, names, and places almost effortlessly; and these recollections turned out to be accurate when I spot-checked them after the interview.

Albert Shanker was perhaps the most remarkable example of an interviewee with near-total recall. When I interviewed him in

March 1993, he was able to close his eyes and recollect the 15 people around a table in 1959 when the first successful teacher's strike was being discussed. When I questioned him about the longest and most controversial union strike in teacher history, the Ocean Hill-Brownsville "Great School War" of 1968, he could recall every politician and union leader who attended each of the major meetings, where he or she sat at the table, and even the major points they made.

After many interviews with educators, I came to expect that a professional educator who had devoted all or most of a career to a topic — such as Seymour Papert with computers and LOGO or Dorothy Rich with home-school education — would be able to recall dozens of details. But I was particularly impressed when noneducators were able to do the same. For example, when I interviewed Rudolph Giuliani in December 1995, he was accompanied by his communications director, Cristyne Lategano. Lategano carried a thick, black, loose-leaf notebook with briefing information on the schools and offered the book to the mayor, who quickly said, "I don't think I'll need it." Throughout the interview, Giuliani supplied precise numbers and percentages for such topics as the graduation rates under varying circumstances, the dropout rate, and the school budget, as well as dozens of names and places. And every fact turned out to be accurate when I checked later.

The third aspect of these interviews that impresses me is the level of idealism and commitment among the interviewees. I can not think of an interviewee who did not volunteer powerful feelings about what he or she was doing. The strength of feeling varied, the degree of idealism varied, but the firm belief in the importance of the work or the rightness of a decision was always there. Sometimes the interviewee made an explicit statement about this. In other cases, the power of the connection to work could be gauged by their decades of devotion.

Seymour Papert talked about how proud he felt after training a group of Costa Rican teachers in LOGO. He had believed for a long time in the efficacy of computers and the specific value of LOGO, but his convictions were confirmed even more deeply when this group of teachers told him they felt their profession and country were affirmed by mastering LOGO – the software program – and the methods used to create the program. Reuven Feuerstein, the Israeli special education leader, stated unequivocally that you can help any human being no matter how badly that person is mentally damaged if you believe deeply in "a moral, affective, emotional engagement with your fellow human being." For Feuerstein, his method for helping learning disabled youngsters is a mission.

Albert Shanker's greatest admiration was for independent thinking that led to bravery in deeds. The 1959 strike of evening-school teachers, the first in the new union's history, created one of the hardest decisions of Shanker's career because he could not be certain of either support or success. He had to believe in the rightness of what he and other union leaders were doing — the belief that this would help to create a strong union that would result in better conditions for teachers and better education for students. When I asked Shanker to elaborate on this commitment, he answered by describing Bayard Rustin from the Civil Rights struggle: "The great thing about Rustin was that he didn't put his finger up to see which way the wind was blowing. He had the guts to say what he felt was right no matter how unpopular it was."

There is one other concern that was shared by almost everyone I interviewed: a deep, and often a primary, interest in the plight of "disadvantaged" youngsters. For example, early in his career Reuven Feuerstein served children who had survived the Holocaust, and later he served any child with a serious learning disability. James Comer and Claudio Sanchez were concerned with children of color, especially children in the inner cities of our nation. And while Don Hirsch was worried about all children, he was concerned mostly with economically deprived children who are inadequately educated both at home and in school.

My interviews will continue; and I am certain from the long, long list of names I have accumulated that I shall not soon run out of people who are determined to ensure that all children will have realistic hope of a high-quality education, opportunities in life, and, ultimately, success.

Photograph by Associated Students UCLA Photography. Used with permission.

Madeline Hunter

Madeline Hunter died in Los Angeles on 28 January 1994 at age 78 after a series of strokes. Dr. Hunter was a whirlwind of activity in education almost to the time of her death. She wrote 12 books and more than 300 articles on teaching and spoke and consulted all over the world. Anyone who ever had the pleasure of hearing her speak knows how well and remarkably she was able to hold the attention of a large audience.

Hunter's particular gift was turning education research and theory into material that classroom teachers can use. Some educators have criticized Dr. Hunter for reducing sophisticated material to relatively simple lists. Other educators have praised her for taking difficult and sometimes indigestible theory and turning it into practical methods. Dr. Hunter's popularity among teachers suggests that the majority of classroom teachers who took her workshops were proud to be "Hunterized."

Over the past 20 years, Madeline Hunter has, in her own words, "spawned an industry." The so-called Hunter model has been presented to tens of thousands of educators concerned with curriculum, research, and teaching. Her "principles of instruction" have been adopted by thousands of teachers and hundreds of school districts across the land. People trained in the model speak of being "Hunterized."

And when they do, they sometimes assume that the model carries the approval of an organization, perhaps UCLA or a Hunter Institute. But, in fact, Hunter works independently, although there are dozens of "Hunter" trainers all over the country, most of whom Hunter herself does not know, some of whom she has trained, and none of whom have any official certification or stamp of recognition.

Originally published as "Portrait of Madeline Hunter" in *Educational Leadership* (February 1990). Used with permission.

Hunter the individual works from the basic convictions about teaching she has developed and modified over her career. She calls her famous model a "teacher decision-making model" and explains that "all of the 5,000 decisions a teacher makes every day fall neatly into three categories: what you're going to teach, which we call a content category; what the students are going to do to learn it and to let you know they've learned it, which we call learning behavior category; and what you as the teacher will do to facilitate and escalate that learning, which is called a teaching behavior category."

She has divided this generic and comprehensive framework into dozens of subcategories as her "translations" of research have progressed. These translations—on such important topics as motivation, retention, anticipatory set, Bloom's Taxonomy of Educational Objectives, hemisphericity, closure, task analysis, and discipline strategies — have produced practical lists and sublists that have great appeal to teachers. And all of this has made her respected, revered, well paid, and sometimes roundly criticized.

Criticisms aside for the moment, Hunter's brilliant achievement prompts a look behind the model at the person whose name has become so famous. My conversation with her provided at least a glimpse.

Pivotal Experiences

When Madeline Hunter was 12 years old, she told me, she sat in a junior high school auditorium waiting to be assigned to her seventh-grade class. The principal stood to read the lists of names for the classes. One by one the names were read, and she watched as most of the best students left the auditorium. She was perplexed, this child who had excelled in six years of elementary school. The principal droned on, and virtually every able student left the auditorium. Hunter cowered in her seat.

Reflecting on that day, Hunter said, "Six years of being successful was destroyed when a person of authority said, 'you're dumb.' I have never forgotten what that can do to a child." She paused, said a few more words about that day, and then stated in a firm, even tone, "You never put a kid down. You always build a kid up."

But the seventh-grade story had a happy ending. Along with 15 other children, Hunter was assigned to an experimental class taught by Christine Cook, who turned out to be a "fantastic teacher and a psychologist." Hunter loved the class, and Cook became her ideal. "Naturally," she said, "I decided as a seventh-grader I was going to be a psychologist."

Hunter went to college and majored in psychology. She recalled, "I was trained impeccably at UCLA as a psychologist. I had the giants of the time training me — Dunlap, Gordon, Gillhausen, Franz — the really great names in psychology at the time." After graduation she continued her training in psychology at Children's Hospital in Los Angeles where, she said, "Ellen Sullivan took me under her wing." This work — often preparing a child and his or her parents for the child's death — she found very depressing. Next she worked at Juvenile Hall, where "at least what those kids had was curable." However, the young psychologist soon found that interventions in that setting were "too little, too late."

The Beginning of a Life Work

"So that I could work at the preventive rather than the remedial end of things," Hunter said, "I decided to become a school psychologist." Going to work for the Inglewood, California, schools, she found the teachers dedicated, intelligent, and even intuitively good in the classroom. But too often, Hunter said, "teachers didn't know much about cause-effect relationships between teaching and learning." They often failed to see relationships between poor behavior and a child's need for attention. Moreover, they didn't ask enough questions, such as why the boy who kept books for his complex counterfeit coin business was failing math in school. And when Hunter asked about "distributing practice" and "massing practice" or mentioned names like Thorndike or Guthrie, no one responded.

"So," she said, "I began working with teachers to translate psychological theory into language a teacher could understand. My mission has been simply to take theory, much of which has been around a hundred years — since Wundt's first consciousness lab — and translate it for classroom teachers."

After 13 years in the Inglewood and Los Angeles City school districts, Hunter became a professor at the University of California at Los Angeles and principal of the UCLA Lab School. Twenty years at the Lab School gave her the time and the place to develop, articulate, and implement her ideas. She continually read research and translated what she read into practice. To illustrate the need for translation, for example, she characterized Benjamin Bloom as a person "whom I admire extravagantly" but added that Bloom did not write for a teacher audience. The researchers "often didn't know what the teacher was facing in the classroom. They're *researchers*. The research is impeccable research done by brilliant people, but it needs translation before it can affect the classroom."

As Hunter's skill at translation became known and appreciated, the use of the translations sometimes became limiting and ritualized. "Because the model has been so successful in helping teachers plan lessons," she explained, "unfortunately it has become a checklist."

Hunter had not anticipated nor intended such effects. She supports the value of translations and at the same time powerfully underscores the infinite complexity and unpredictability of teaching: "When you're working with humans, you're always working with probabilities, never certainties, and there are always exceptions." She has come to understand that "teaching is an action performance behavior like music, like dancing, like athletics, like surgery. You have to automate many behaviors so you can perform them artistically at high speed."

The Requirements of Artistry

When Hunter talked about artistry in teaching, she explained the program's limitations and its frequent modifications, which one must understand before it can be internalized, and she peppered her remarks with colorful metaphors. When I asked her about the sameness in lessons based on checklists, she pointed out that both the Taj Mahal and the Lincoln Memorial use principles of parallel lines and symmetry "but do not look alike." She added, "People aren't used to looking at underlying principles." At one point, in some exasperation, she said, "I am now on a one-woman broom all over the world saying there is absolutely nothing you should expect to see in every lesson and nothing you have to do in education — except *think*." She kept emphasizing many routes to the same goal; for example, "Raw fish, dried caribou, and peanut soup are all proteins. They're all going to give you good protein." When I questioned her about the currency of her ideas, she used the continual refinements of cardiac bypass surgery as her example to illustrate evolutionary development within a profession. She was anxious, through these examples, to defend her basic model as she presents it and not as it has been represented or misrepresented in articles or classrooms.

If you look at Hunter's work, the reason for the "misunderstandings" is apparent, even graphic. *Seven* factors to increase motivation, *six* attributes of an effective example, or *five* characteristics of retention — these lists are eminently useful, even seductive. However, it may be more a comment on inservice education than on the Hunter model that so many educators have taken the model to task for being inflexible and limiting. Hunter was quick to point out that the necessary training in her model should take at least two years of dedicated work, not two hours of lecture with two handouts for follow-up.

Hunter used the example of her own ballet training to show how internalized learning happens. As a teenager, she "fell in love with ballet." But it took years to learn to dance well, to make dance a natural part of her being. And it was hard work. "My ballet training stood me in good stead. For one thing, I learned that rigor undergirds artistic performance."

Rigor and time are the two things she requires if a school district is to take her model seriously. "Two months is a drop in the bucket in terms of what we know about learning." Districts must send their staff members to valid workshops time and time again, provide continual support in the home district, and send the trainees back for research updates as often as possible. "If you don't have time for follow-up, you're wasting my time and your money," she asserts.

But she is quick to accept part of the blame for inadequate training; for example, she said, "One of the egregious errors on my part is that when I was teaching principles of learning, I never taught under what conditions you should *not* use them." She explained that if a student should make a very perceptive remark, there are conditions under which it should not be reinforced, even though positive reinforcement is usually desirable. She said, "If it's blurted out, or if it's going to move the class in an unproductive direction, or if this is a shy boy who can't stand public approval, a kid who's looked upon as a brain, when reinforcement from the teacher will alienate him further from the group, or if it's a kid who habitually does this, I would not reinforce the remark."

As Demanding as Surgery

Justifiably proud of her accomplishments, Hunter recalled a few indicators of the quality and popularity of her work. "Teachers from the Lab School have graduated into superintendents, principals, directors of inservice; several of them are freelance consultants." She points with satisfaction to her efforts in the inner-city Los Angeles school that improved to the satisfaction of the California State Department of Education and of independent researcher Rod Skager. She cites with equal pride her work in such disparate places as Wilmette, Illinois, and San Bernardino, California. Hunter remains in demand all over the country. Each January, from the 500 or more requests she receives to speak or to do workshops, she selects commitments for the following year. She takes special pride in the teachers who return to her workshops to increase their skills and the districts that apply her ideas with integrity.

Repeatedly in our conversation, Hunter mentioned complexity: "I hope I live to see public recognition of the incredible complexity of teaching." Most people believe "teaching is just telling kids what to do and maintaining discipline." Hunter believes it's more like surgery, "where you think fast on your feet and do the best you can with the information you have. You must be very skilled, very knowledgeable, and exquisitely well trained, because neither the teacher nor the surgeon can say, 'Everybody sit still until I figure out what in the heck we're gonna do next'."

I asked Hunter what she hopes people will say years from now about her influence. Without a pause she replied, "If I could have my wish, I would hope my work would help move teaching from a craft to a profession based on research translated into artistic practice, where the professional is a decision maker and where that professional never stops learning."

Photograph by Donna Coveney, Massachusetts Institute of Technology. Used with permission.

Seymour Papert

I heard Seymour Papert speak at a conference in Boston in the mid-1980s and was impressed with what he had to say about computers and education, though I thought he was an academic visionary whose predictions might come true in 30 or 40 years, but certainly not in 10. The wealthiest and most progressive schools in the country were just beginning to warm to the idea of the personal computer. Most educators, myself included, could not believe that computers soon would be in almost every school, let alone be in tens of millions of American homes. Of course, Papert was right and I was wrong. I found out why when I visited him in his office at MIT in Cambridge, Massachusetts.

One of the first things Papert showed me at MIT was the work he and his staff were doing on LOGO, the program designed to make computers accessible to children. I watched graduate students manipulate plastic building blocks robotically using the LOGO program, nothing new today, but stunning in the fall of 1990 when I visited Papert. I soon understood that MIT had prototypes for just about everything that was to happen in high technology in the next decade or two.

Incidentally, the part of Papert's mid-1980s lecture that seemed the most pie-in-the-sky to me is today called the Palm Pilot.

Seymour Papert, the father of the programming language LOGO, is a pensive, soft-spoken man. A bit over 60, he has a light South African accent and tousled salt-and-pepper hair and beard; he prefers to dress informally. He uses "perhaps" a great deal in his speech and tries to be careful and balanced in all that he says. His modest, relaxed appearance belies his importance in education: for 25 years he has been a pioneer in connecting computers to schools and learning. His brainchild, LOGO, is present

Originally published as "Portrait of Seymour Papert" in *Educational Leadership* (April 1991). Used with permission.

in at least one-third of American elementary classrooms and has expanded internationally, reaching as far as small towns in Latin America and rural schools in the Soviet Union.

Life in Africa

Papert's father was an entymologist who studied the tsetse fly — that bloodsucking African insect which carries pathogenic parasites to humans and livestock. Before DDT, the only way to escape tsetse fly invasions was to predict their movement in order to avoid them. During the early 1930s, young Seymour spent months each year in "various wild places on the southeast coast of Africa" with his parents, their white assistant, and several black workers and their families.

It was in this "transparent little world" that Papert became interested in learning the mechanics of things. He recalls how as a small boy he once drove a truck two miles an hour, hit a tree, and jumped out of the stalled truck, wild with excitement to see how the gears worked. In this environment Papert's lifelong desire flourished — he always wanted to figure out "how physical things worked — but also how minds work."

The family moved to a permanent home in Pretoria; Papert entered school and "hit into segregationist South Africa." His logical mind and his familiarity with black people had left him without any racist stain. From his earliest memory, he says, "the racist thinking in South Africa seemed to me not only wrong, but profoundly unintelligible, mysterious."

When he was a schoolboy of 11 or 12, Seymour and three other boys, seeing the need for local black workers to learn how to read and to function in modern society, decided to lobby the administration of their school for an evening course of studies for blacks. The administration turned them down flat, so Papert and his friends organized a meeting of their parents. Simply assuming that their successful and respected mothers and fathers would apply pressure on the administration, they were astonished, recalls Papert, "that the parents supported the administration. The main argument was

'You can't have these people come here to our schools; they'll bring disease.' These were the same people who were the cooks in their houses and the nursemaids of their children."

The boys sensed that the stated argument wasn't the real reason for keeping the blacks illiterate, and they were disturbed "that people could stand up and give this sort of argument and not be ashamed." Papert, who early in life had grasped the workings of a gear, could not fathom this "total irrationality." In this incident he now sees the "roots in my interest in philosophy of mind and the theory of intelligence. From the beginning it was tied up with an activist streak."

Mathematics, practical activism, and philosophy merged in Papert's mind as he widened his experiences and studies. At South Africa's Witwatersrand University, he was attracted to mathematics, but only partially because of its content and structure; he also understood how powerfully mathematics related to philosophy. And part of the reason he had chosen mathematics as a course of study was because he saw it as a politically neutral subject at a time when his college activism kept him in trouble in South Africa.

Work with Piaget: Understanding Learning

In 1959 Jean Piaget invited Papert to work with him in Geneva. Piaget was studying how children begin to understand mathematics, and he was impressed with Papert's doctoral thesis on the understanding of topology as pure mathematics. To uncover the learning process, Piaget felt, "you really have to understand the deepest questions about the nature of mathematics." It followed then, Piaget said, that "mathematicians and especially people interested in the philosophy of mathematics are more important to have around than psychologists." His work with Piaget convinced Papert that it was more interesting to study what children can do than what they cannot do. The way to change education was not in concentrating on any particular technique but to change the entire culture in which education takes place.

The Cyprus Epiphany

In 1965, walking on a hilltop in Cyprus, Papert realized — "it just sort of hit me like a thunderbolt" — that computers had great potential for making a difference in our culture. The best way to contribute to education would be to "harness that cultural change to the lives of children, the growth of children."

This insight led him to the National Physics Laboratory in England, where he could use "the biggest computer in Europe." While learning to program and to think about computers and learning, he began to meet people from MIT, notably Warren McCulloch and Marvin Minsky. His association with them caused him to deepen his Piagetian belief "that children are builders of their own intellectual structures." At the same time, he pondered the paradox Piaget had voiced: children are marvelous at learning, and yet in school it seems so difficult to teach them.

The MIT Years

Through his association with Piaget, Papert had found "a way of putting together these two poles of mathematics: philosophy of mind and a way that could have an activist facet, that could lead to rethinking how children learn and change the nature of education perhaps." Soon Papert joined the computer revolution at MIT and began to use computers to change the culture of education.

When he first arrived at MIT, he found "there weren't any people here involved in research on children, so for a while that aspect was eclipsed, and I concentrated on theoretical models of intelligence and artificial intelligence." By 1967, he was hard at work on his mission, although at the time people "put down what I was proposing as accessible only to the rich and privileged." Papert understood that the first personal computers would soon be available to the public and he wanted to make it possible for children to master the computer. Describing the early drill-and-practice uses of computers as "the computer programming the child," he sought to create a computer microworld, not unlike the fascinating world of his father's research camp in Swaziland: a world that a child could master.

So he created LOGO to make the computer accessible to children. "The spirit," he says, "is to make the computer an expressive medium for a child to use in a natural way, in a way that's like a producer, not a consumer. For instance, children see animated cartoons all the time "but they have little opportunity to make their own. The computer as an instrument can allow children to make animated pictures — then tell a story in action and movement on a screen by programming the computer."

The computer has logical rules, but Papert has shown they can be applied in multiple and creative ways. He speaks constantly of "opportunities," "multiple paths," and "masterful use." His desire is to "as far as possible put the user in charge . . . and to avoid having arbitrary rules imposed by the design of software."

Today's Projects

Education research is now the center of Papert's work. One important project is at Hennigan Elementary School, a typical "inner-city Boston public school" — 30% black and 30% Hispanic. Unlike his prior projects in which only enthusiastic teachers volunteered to participate, the Hennigan project includes all the teachers in the school. "We've taken a group of 18 teachers in an inner-city public school. They're mostly women, average age well up in the 40s. We've made them learn to program. We've asked a lot from them in terms of time — summer activities, one afternoon a week, lunchtime meetings. No one's ever dropped out because they didn't want to learn this stuff." This is a LOGO-Lego project, one of the newest applications for LOGO. Lego is "something children know about outside of school and have a lot of skills in." The goal is to build a computer culture in the school that has "roots in the general culture." Students in Hennigan School are learning in their computer-enriched environment. Computers are in classrooms; they are not restricted to a centralized computer lab. The teachers constantly "look for ways of making connections" using LOGO-Lego. Students learn design, physics, math, and mechanics. They learn computer programming fundamentals when they build Lego structures — not simulations but actual structures — using Lego pieces, motors, gears, and sensors. A Lego robot on a magnetic track actually builds structures on computer command.

Another of Papert's efforts is a computers-in-the-schools program in Costa Rica, based entirely on using LOGO. President Oscar Arias made the project part of his platform when he ran for office and is determined to carry it through. Before beginning the project, Papert asked the Costa Ricans to consider whether they wanted to adopt a program that would be very easy for the teachers to implement (put a diskette in the machine and have software that would run pretty well automatically without any effort from the teacher) or whether they wanted to require the teachers to really learn the computer. Costa Rica opted for the second alternative and sent teachers to MIT for a three-week experiment: They came, they learned, and they mastered the computer. To Papert, "they were spectacular. It was an affirmation of their country, it was an affirmation of their profession — not a low-grade profession that can't contribute anything sophisticated — and since many of them were women, it was an affirmation of their gender, too."

Through LOGO, Papert has realized his dream of making children masterful users of computers and providing them with many ways to solve problems, including some that have never occurred to him. When I asked him for his thoughts on why LOGO is so deeply appealing to children, he paused, as always, to think for a moment. Then he replied, "many schools appear to kids as a look to the past. This is a piece of the space age that you can hold in your hand. It's a connection with what you see on the television set; it's a connection with the future."

Reuven Feuerstein

Reuven Feuerstein, in his late 60's when I interviewed him in 1991, looked like a biblical prophet with his grand white beard and ever-present dark beret. He often is treated like a biblical figure and has the bearing of one. I interviewed Feuerstein in the first-class lounge of El Al Airlines in New York and later at his institute in a quiet Jerusalem neighborhood. At El Al, there were several families waiting to see the "great man," parents with severely disabled children who wanted to implore him to work one of his "miracles" on their child. I later learned that people find Feuerstein wherever he is.

In Jerusalem, we got to the heart of Feuerstein's work. He emphasized over and over again that this is not ordinary work, not a job, but a sacred mission to save children whom most people consider beyond redemption. He told me that what he and his staff do requires absolute conviction in the amelioration of undeveloped children no matter how badly damaged they appear to be. Fervent, persistent, and informed adult mediation based on years of research and experience can create impressive improvement in any child. While some children are more resistant to adult mediation than others, almost every child progresses, some quite dramatically, if they remain with Feuerstein or his trained staff for a year or two.

Reuven Feuerstein has been touched by history. He has the bearing of an Old Testament figure, this aging practitioner/philosopher/scholar, with his oversize black beret, ready smile, insistent personality, and long, triangular, pristine white beard. Born into a poor but dignified family in Rumania, he spent his young manhood on a personal adventure that took him from a Nazi concentration camp to the back alleys of Bucharest to Israel,

Originally published as "Portrait of Reuven Feuerstein" in *Educational Leadership* (September 1991). Used with permission.

Switzerland, France, and Morocco. He survived tuberculosis in a time when most died from it. He has spent his life working with ruined people, most often children suffering from poverty, cultural deprivation, disease — often victims of a society gone mad.

For nearly 50 years Feuerstein has worked with troubled youngsters, children from 70 distinct cultures, children considered not educable in any meaningful way. He has traveled throughout the world to meet children and work with them, and children have come from all over the Earth to him. At first he worked with Holocaust survivors; later he worked with mentally and emotionally afflicted youngsters and children who were severely culturally deprived. "Whoever would see such children," Feuerstein remembers, "would immediately stigmatize and categorize them as impaired, organically damaged, genetically disordered — you name it. These children were considered mentally defective."

But Feuerstein's irrepressible optimism steered him clear of despair; it allowed him to "center himself internally and form himself" into a person who could work with children and young adults and "see those children come out of the most terrible conditions to develop and mature and become able to function." One boy named Leror was unable to function after being rescued from a concentration camp. For three days he had been buried under "tons of corpses." With Feuerstein's intervention he not only survived but became a healthy person who developed interests in music and poetry. An autistic Italian boy he worked with, who would often "freeze for 10 minutes," is now an optician who plays classical music as his hobby. Time and again, Feuerstein has nourished hope in children considered retarded or autistic, helping them grow into fully functioning adults.

Taking Children "Beyond Themselves"

Rather than pronounce such children hopeless cases, Feuerstein held a different perspective. "I consider these children modifiable. I don't have to categorize them in a way that will immediately place them in an environment for subnormal individuals." They may need encouragement and mediation that will allow them to move into the normal culture, but rarely are they hopeless.

Modifiability is the essential and undergirding tenet of Feuerstein's program. Feuerstein sees human intelligence as a plastic quality — not fixed. Many specialists assess a child's ability and conclude, he says, that "the child doesn't have abstract thinking. With this they close all the roads toward changing him. Well, we just don't accept it. *Why* doesn't he have abstract thinking? What is hampering the child?" Feuerstein has looked at children with IQs in the low 60s, epileptics, children who were labeled autistic, children who were rated imbeciles, and determined that these children could be modified. The basic question he asks himself when he meets a troubled child is "What are the chances that this child can go beyond himself?"

An adult intervenor must offer purposeful direction, an approach Feuerstein refers to as mediated learning. It is not enough to provide a child with books and music; an adult must help the child to interpret and make sense of the materials, so the child can "go beyond himself." When a skilled adult tells a child about types of plants or trees, he is also helping the child to group, to make distinctions, to appreciate, to notice — to do all sorts of things that include, but also go beyond, technical knowledge of learning (method) and what Feuerstein calls instrumental enrichment (IE – the use of specific materials and exercises) that the youngster learns to organize, to see similarities and differences, to plan – to do the hundreds of things that promote effective learning.

In an anecdote worthy of a Zen master, Feuerstein posed a question to me: "What makes a cup of tea sweet — the sugar or the spoon? It's a very difficult question. If it is the sugar, why do you need the spoon? If it is the spoon, why do you need the sugar? The truth is that it is the spoon that makes the tea sweet. Why do you need the sugar? So the spoon will have what to mix."

You may give the child books and tapes and educational games (sugar); but unless the adult provides hints, guidance, some direction (spoon), the tea (child's growth) will not become sweet. The child's independence must be respected, but it is in the nature of the adult-child relationship that the spoon must be put to skillful use or little sweetness will occur.

A Different Kind of Assessment

Feuerstein's method of assessment is revealing. His Learning Potential Assessment Device (LPAD), rather than simply accepting the level of the individual's functioning as a predictor of how well he or she will always function, actually "produces changes in the individual — structural changes — which we consider a sample of the possible changes that can be produced in an individual — namely, modifiability." To watch the LPAD being administered is to watch a dialogue, a tutorial. The tester and testee interact to determine how the child learns and how and what the child might learn. The test includes hints, directions, questions — most of them framed at that moment by the highly trained tester.

The LPAD can take several days and up to 25 hours to administer. When youngsters are examined, the tester coaches the child to understand such concepts as right- or left-handedness or time. After 10 or 15 or more hours, it becomes clear how the child learns, what his deficiencies are, and what techniques might be useful in modifying him.

It is not easy to accept the revelations of this dynamic test. "You have to see it, experience it in order to understand it," Feuerstein explains. Take, for example, the case of a boy who is unable to attend to any task for more than two minutes. He has been labeled an epileptic with an IQ of 63. After testing him, Feuerstein says, "It turns out that we have a boy with an IQ of 158. He showed a capacity to learn with such rapidity. I gave him a very difficult attention test. He completed it with one error and with maximum precision."

A Family Tradition of Service

The wellspring of Feuerstein's belief in these children resides in his individual passion: "You must believe that human beings can be changed. If you are really engaged emotionally as a human being, you will say, 'I have to. I must help. Change is possible because I want it so urgently'."

Reuven Feuerstein's passion was nurtured in his childhood home by parents who took learning and helping others seriously. As a boy growing up in the small town of Botoshany, Rumania, he would read his mother's *Book of Prayers,* which was filled with history, poetry, legends, stories, and wisdom. Most important to Feuerstein, it was a "book salted with tears," a lesson in passion.

Feuerstein had eight siblings and slept in a room with four brothers. "In the middle of the room," he recalls, "was a table, and on the table was a little oil lamp." At 5:00 a.m. his father would light the lamp and walk around the table saying his prayers, "and his sweet voice was waking us up."

His father was a counselor to the town's Jews, a man who made his home a center of family life, learning, and respect. "My father was the most powerful image," Feuerstein remembers. "People were literally standing at the door to get advice. This image had a strong impact on me." His father died in 1943. Reuven, then 22 years old, could not get to the funeral from Bucharest because the Nazis were in power. He had already spent one year in a working concentration camp in Transylvania. To go to another town, "you had to get all kinds of permits, permits from the police." Young Feuerstein, engaged in anti-Nazi activities and an effort to flee Europe, could not risk the encounter.

A Move to Israel

In 1944 Feuerstein escaped from a brief second captivity and made his way to Israel. In Europe he had worked as a counselor and teacher with orphaned children of Holocaust victims, but with little advanced training and under terrible conditions. When he got to Israel, he went to a kibbutz, where he had an experience that was to be a turning point in his career. When the members of the kibbutz held an assembly to discuss a five-year plan, he realized the value of goal-setting. "I came from a place where you couldn't plan more than a minute. It was a real culture shock. I learned to teach children to plan."

For the next four years, Feuerstein worked with children who had survived the Holocaust, Soviet youngsters, and culturally deprived children from Persia and Morocco. All needed a transition to a normal culture. During this period, Feuerstein "started to examine the great question of human modifiability. . . . Are there ways to modify individuals?"

A Brush with Death

But before he could really get started on this path of inquiry, he contracted tuberculosis and was sent to a sanitarium. Pronounced incurable, he went to a Swiss sanitarium seeking a final determination. Both lungs were affected, and the Swiss specialist said definitively, "We can't help you."

The prospect of death taught Feuerstein a second great lesson: You do not have to accept conventional wisdom. The power of human belief is enormous. Feuerstein fervently "believed that I would make it. I wanted to live." So he simply harnessed the will to return to health and "disobeyed my doctors and went to study and work."

For the next seven years, he worked with children in Europe and Israel and studied in Geneva with Piaget, Inhelder, and Andre Rey. "During this period," he recalls, "I learned the essence of human modifiability and went beyond it to sketch a whole series of outlines for a theory that later became known as the Theory of Structural Cognitive Modifiability." He regained his health, then went on to establish his world-famous clinic in Israel in 1955, the Hadassah Research Institute.

Working with Down's Syndrome Youths

Now Feuerstein is applying his philosophy and techniques to Down's Syndrome youngsters. "You should see the Down's Syndrome children learning to become companions to the elderly. They undergo a training period of 18 months: They learn to cook, to buy, they learn to live totally independently."

The Down's Syndrome youngsters receive training during the day, but in the evening they stay in youth hostels with normal children from all over the world. "They meet with them at the table, talk to them, interact with them, making some nervous with their questions. They interact in a way that will make them sense reality, react to reality, cope with reality, and be modified by reality." He worked very hard to close down the specialized environments for these children, where they were isolated from normal people — "It took me about nine years," he recalls.

A Program for American Schools

In placing handicapped children in normal environments, Feuerstein feels, educators in the United States have had only modest success. He believes that American teachers do not yet have sufficient passion for working with afflicted children. "There is great interest, a readiness on the part of teachers. I do not always feel there is the spirit of urgency." It is not enough to train children for a few hours a day; he feels the work must be done with deep belief. And the children must spend a great deal of time in a normal environment.

Feuerstein believes the United States needs a visionary training program to completely integrate specialized and mainstreamed education. Teachers must "mediate the prerequisites of learning, of thinking, of behavior, of motivation, of self-image, of emotional affective ties that will enable the individual to benefit from existence in a normative environment."

For the past decade, Feuerstein has invested a great deal of energy in Curriculum Development Associates, an organization headed by Frances Link. "Our major target is not the child only, but the teacher first and then the child. I consider the training more important than the program." Teachers must come to believe firmly "that you can change people, that you can affect an individual meaningfully. It's not just training in a program. It's training in a whole philosophy, a whole way of looking at a child."

"I Cannot Give Up"

Although he will be 70 this year, Feuerstein has neither reduced his work week nor stopped seeing children. "I am seeing almost daily three or four children," he says. But increasingly he is putting his energy into writing about his program, sponsoring training programs, and getting people interested in his work. He wants to teach others his belief system and practices so that his work may outlive him. The elements of his program have taken 50 years to refine, and he expects that they will undergo continual change. There is one constant, however, that this latter-day prophet presents as his refrain: "If you don't believe that human beings are modifiable, it's partly because you don't really need to modify them. You don't have a moral, affective, emotional engagement with your fellow human which will make you say, 'No, I cannot give up. It's not something I can give up.'"

Shirley Brice Heath

Shirley Brice Heath is a woman of great dignity and charm, someone I noticed immediately when she entered the room where I was doing a workshop in San Francisco. We had agreed to meet for her interview just after my presentation. She would know me because I was at the podium, but I knew who she was as soon as the tall, slim, graceful woman with white-gray hair and the extremely alert, intelligent face strode into the room.

Shirley is a linguist, so I should not have been surprised at her voice. She can speak with the bearing and confidence of the highly educated and accomplished person she is. But she can, and often does, fall into the voice of her childhood or the people she's interviewed over the years in impoverished communities, an affectless technique that lends great credibility to everything Shirley says, as well as makes the interview more interesting because you don't know just which authentic voices you may be privileged to hear. It is a grand opportunity to hear first the voice of the educated professor and then, say, the voices of communities in the Carolinas where Shirley lived and did research.

Few educators can claim the breadth of experience of Shirley Brice Heath. As an anthropologist, linguist, and social historian, she has studied diverse communities in the United States and Latin America and has written on topics ranging from government language policies to the importance of reading bedtime stories to children. She has taught in elementary and secondary schools, as well as at the university level. Audiences on five continents have heard her describe her work, which she approaches with passion and commitment. Her work has influenced many educators who want to know how language acquisition, family

Originally published as "Portrait of Shirley Brice Heath" in *Educational Leadership* (April 1992). Used with permission.

practices, community myths, local customs, and public policy influence the way children learn and make life choices in school.

The recipient of the David H. Russell Award for Distinguished Research in language arts and a MacArthur Foundation creativity award, Heath was elected to the National Academy of Education in 1990. She is currently professor of English and linguistics at Stanford University, with courtesy appointments in anthropology and education.

A Lifelong Study Unfolds

These exemplary accomplishments belie Heath's humble beginnings in rural southern Virginia and western North Carolina. As she puts it, her early life was "atypical of most people who end up working with language. . . . I did not grow up with a rich literary background." Heath spent much of her early life with her grandmother, who had an eighth-grade education, or with a foster mother. Many of Heath's friends were black. She describes herself as someone who "grew up speaking black English with a Southern white, lower-class accent."

A new world opened up to Heath when, in her early teens, she spent a summer in Indiana with her aunt and uncle. "My father's sister married a man who had gone to Harvard Law School, and they were the ones who really gave me a sense of myself." She spent the summer "experiencing books and people who talked about ballet and concerts," and she returned to high school "with the idea to take opportunities, to take risks, to stay out of the standard track."

But Heath's childhood circumstances had left a lasting imprint, giving her the instinct and the impetus to do ethnographic work in low-income areas. She characterizes much of her work as being "focused on the lives, the language, and the cultural backgrounds of minority populations, or what you might call 'subordinated populations'."

During the late 1950s and early 1960s, Heath worked in Mississippi with poor blacks and in California with migrant workers.

In Mississippi, mostly in Biloxi, she worked with some music and art groups, "the rural equivalent of street theater." As a result of her work in Southern California, Heath, fluent in Spanish, realized that children of migrant workers were put in special education classes because they couldn't speak English.

In 1962, after interrupting college several times to work at various jobs and having attended five schools, Heath received her A.B. degree from Lynchburg College in Virginia. She graduated with an inchoate understanding that "many poor kids are broken and turn to drugs and alcohol as substitutes for self-esteem."

Heath lived with her aunt and uncle again while doing graduate work at Ball State. After completing her work there, her growing interests in Spanish, Latin American culture, linguistics, anthropology, and English as a second language led her to Columbia University. Her area of concentration was Latin American culture with a focus on anthropology, and she did fieldwork in Mexico and Guatemala. By now, she was married and had two small children. Unwilling to be less than a full-time mother, she took her children to Mexico while she did her fieldwork there. Soon after receiving her doctorate in 1970, she published her first book, *Telling Tongues: Language Policy in Mexico — Colony to Nation.*

Between 1970 and 1980, Heath taught at several Southern colleges, got divorced, raised her children, and married her current husband, Charles Ferguson, a Stanford linguist. She also completed fieldwork in the Carolinas for *Ways With Words,* a description of ethnographic research in the Piedmont area from 1969 to 1978.

Throughout her career, most of Heath's efforts have been "youth related." She has raised such issues as "how the uses of language and the daily habits of valuing and arranging time and space could tell us something about how schools and other institutions that affect young people might work differently." She also has reacted against the powerful assimilationist and behaviorist impulses of the 1950s and 1960s "to shape young people out of their indigenous patterns and habits." By fostering appreciation of different cultures and their language socialization patterns, Heath believed she could offer schools and other institutions options for working with minority populations that would capitalize on the unique backgrounds and talents of these children. Her bedrock belief has been that "we should have schools that acknowledge these kids as resources rather than problems."

When I asked Heath about the language of the lower-class rural children she studied, she responded:

> They do not have baby talk directed at them. They're never asked questions to which the adults already know the answer. In contrast, mainstream middle-class children are constantly asked, "Where is your nose?" or told, "Point to Daddy." If a middle-class child pulls on an adult's pant leg, the result is, "Yes, Susie, what is it?" Susie gets the conversational floor. That just wouldn't happen in a working-class rural family. It's unthinkable.

Yet these working-class children have a wide range of functions of language and can sustain long utterances. They are particularly good at imitation, from the styles of radio voices to those "of the old man who lives down the road when he's sober and when he's drunk." The mainstream child "can tell a story on demand: 'Tell Daddy what you did today, Danny'."

The mainstream skill, of course, is more valued in school. The poor rural child is perceived as a "nugget of potential that needs love and nurturing to unfold." The middle-class child, also loved, benefits from substantial adult mediation and mentoring, a factor that Heath understands well from her relationship with her own aunt and uncle.

While much of Heath's work is technical — "analysis of syntax, discourse features, genres, hypotheticals, and conditionals" — both she and her results capture the essence of human behavior. More than once when Heath summarized a particular event or made a point, she spoke in the precise accent or dialect of a person she had talked with, revealing in an unaffected way her total immersion in her work.

What Makes a Difference for Urban Youth?

In the mid-1980s, a few years after joining the faculty at Stanford, Heath began studying neighborhood-based organizations in three major U.S. cities. She wanted to know why these organizations had success with many disadvantaged youngsters. She had begun her research with the question, "If we were to look at a sampling of kids from desperate circumstances who 'made it,' what would we find as the one or two factors that made a difference?" In every case, she discovered, there was a mentor, an individual who said, "You've got some great potential, and I'll help you." Often, she found, the mentor was connected to a local youth organization. The second factor she identified was "sustained involvement with some sort of neighborhood-based organization beyond the family that gave the young person a wider set of models."

For many urban youth, the neighborhood organizations are places to do theater, to box, to play basketball — short-term, engaging activities. The surrounding neighborhood is full of peril, but these organizations are what Heath calls "fortresses against the rest of the world. . . and within them, kids are safe."

Neighborhood-based organizations are not only safe, but also reassuring. Rules are very few: "No drugs" or "Leave this place the way you found it." The list of rooms tells youngsters exactly the choices they have: sculpture, boxing, pool, library, homework, drama. Uplifting mottos adorn the walls. Heath points out that "many of the leaders of these groups are kids themselves — just a little older" and experienced in the activity.

Some of Heath's work in neighborhood organizations has benefited young people in unexpected ways. For example, some of the youngsters in the organizations she is studying showed an interest in Heath's field notes, and a few have even volunteered to be junior ethnographers. "We do a lot of orienting of these youngsters to the ethics of recording the language of others. We make sure they know we are not interested in recording drug deals or plans for robberies. We just want to know what kind of language they use when they get together and talk about what happens." Some of the junior ethnographers liked what they were doing enough to transfer that enthusiasm to school and then to go on to college.

When I questioned Heath about the role of teachers and schools in low-income neighborhoods, she answered cautiously and thoughtfully, saying there are some fine teachers, but for many kids, school is not the central answer. Most of these kids are absolutely convinced that they can't learn in school and "know that the work world is the only real world." Teachers often

> cannot overcome the generally repressive ethos of schools for these kids. Many of them go to schools in the worst part of town; they're in schools that are not always able to recruit the teachers of greatest imagination — and if they do, there are very repressive environments for these teachers, very limited resources. The kids and the teachers struggle against a lot of odds. Very few of the kids connect schools to their lives.

Many of Heath's findings published nearly a decade ago in *Ways with Words* have recently leached into the mainstream of education thought. For example, Heath learned that "the work world demands that you display knowledge nonverbally, that you display in an array of ways what you know, and that you have some strong potential for self-assessment." She found that "working in teams is valuable" and that "learning from mistakes, [though] not very valued in schools, is highly valued in the workplace."

Heath also understands the importance of schools and families working together. She is aware, however, that no single or monolithic solution will work; language patterns, racial and ethnic differences, family practices, economic disparities, and dozens of other issues come into play.

Discovering Questions, Seeking Answers

While Heath's influence has been considerable among people who know her work, she asserts that she is not "a problem solver for education" and says she is "repelled by university people coming to tell those of us who have spent so many hours in the classroom what to do with our kids."

Clearly there will never be a Shirley Brice Heath method. She sees life as far too complex for that and is more interested in working with teachers to help them find ways of discovering questions, patterns, and answers that might fit their idiosyncratic circumstances. "I don't give answers; I search for answers. I have lots of questions, but very few answers to anything."

Heath's passion for her work continues unabated. Her interests range from the role of voice in American literature to the continuing work on youth organizations. Her commitment to low-income children is now centered on college training:

> One of our best hopes for increasing and enhancing the opportunity for children of subordinated cultures and languages is to have more and more people in colleges who have the sensibility and the teaching experience necessary to understand minority children. They also must be people who are willing to take the relevant social science and linguistic and historical knowledge and bring that to bear on thinking about how institutions and policy work.

Heath's amalgam of scholarship, research, perseverance, optimism, and sheer hard work, buttressed by the belief that every dedicated mentor can make an important difference, keeps her work alive and influential.

Albert Shanker

A month after Albert Shanker died on 22 February 1997, a memorial ceremony attended by 2,000 people was held at New York's Lincoln Center. Such distinguished people as Senator Edward M. Kennedy and former New York Mayor Edward I. Koch spoke about Shanker's impressive contribution to the labor movement and human rights.

A gifted speaker and writer, the long-time president of New York City's 85,000-member United Federation of Teachers and its parent organization, the 900,000-member American Federation of Teachers, Shanker was remembered as one of this country's most powerful, caring, and effective union leaders. During the two decades of his national prominence, Shanker was an eloquent and forceful spokesperson for teachers, children, civil rights, and international cooperation.

Shanker was 68 years old when he died at Memorial Sloan-Kettering Hospital in Manhattan after a three-year battle with bladder cancer. By 1973, Shanker was already known well enough to be satirized in Woody Allen's comedy "Sleeper." In his later years, he became an intimate of presidents ranging from Lech Walesa of Poland to Presidents Bush and Clinton of the United States.

Albert Shanker's quintessential New Yorker qualities — brashness, informality, social awareness, and volubility — are known far and wide. His career has taken him many places — to visit such world figures as Lech Walesa and Vaclav Havel, to meet with mayors and governors, and even, with some frequency, to visit the Oval Office. As long-time president of the American Federation of Teachers, Shanker has the ear of cabinet secretaries, U.S. senators, and members of Congress, as well as leading business people and heads of state of other countries. But

Originally published as "A Portrait of Albert Shanker" in *Educational Leadership* (March 1993). Used with permission.

these are images of Al Shanker today. What forces and events shaped the person that he is now?

A Budding Social Conscience

New York City in the 1930s and 1940s was home to Al Shanker. When Shanker started school, he spoke no English. His parents — Yiddish-speaking immigrants from then-Czarist Russia — instilled in young Albert a love of the United States with their frequent stories of how bad things were in "the Old Country."

Shanker did not have to look far to see harsh conditions in his own surroundings. His mother, a garment worker, worked a 75-hour week. His father, too, worked long hours every day. Starting at 2:00 a.m., he delivered morning and evening papers behind a pushcart.

Growing up in this era inspired a social conscience in young Shanker. He recalls that at age eight, he "went to a Roosevelt headquarters to get leaflets and buttons to distribute." In the late 1930s, Father Coughlin's anti-Semitic radio program was popular in his neighborhood, and strong premonitions of what was about to happen in Europe pervaded the community. At 12, Shanker joined various interventionist committees that supported the entry of the United States into the war against Hitler.

Shortly before the United States entered World War II, Shanker joined the Boy Scout troop in a nearby housing project and experienced his first taste of leadership. Before long, he presented a petition to the scoutmaster, urging that the way the troop was run be changed. Later, when the scoutmaster was drafted for military service, he asked 14-year-old Shanker — bright, tough-minded, and already over six feet — to take over. Running the troop of 30 to 70 youngsters gave Shanker a model for how to run an educational program "where kids didn't have to sit still and be quiet and listen to somebody."

A Strong Voice for Teachers

In 1952, after completing college at the University of Illinois and three years of graduate school at Columbia University,

Shanker began teaching. His salary, including a differential for graduate work, was $2,400. In New York City at that time, there was no powerful teachers' union, not even the hint of collective bargaining. There were 106 small teacher organizations, some ideological, others educational, and a few largely social. Teachers had no lunch or duty-free period, and class size was more than 40 students. After-school meetings were at the whim of the principal, and the hottest topic in Shanker's school was the size of the gift for the principal at the end-of-year party.

It was at this point that Shanker's mother — a long-time member of the Amalgamated Clothing and Textile Workers Union of America and the International Ladies' Garment Workers Union, put things into perspective for him. "Even in the sweat shop, we have time for lunch. You teachers are supposed to be so smart, but you're dumb not to have a union."

In 1952, the Condon Wadlin Act barred public employees from striking; the prevailing attitude toward authority was a "general feeling of helplessness." Shanker recalled that many years later, in a terrible confrontation over race, he watched a heated debate between a racially mixed faculty and the superintendent of schools: "Tears came to my eyes because I never thought I'd live to see the day when teachers who have been so frightened of authority would take on the superintendent."

All through the 1950s, Shanker taught and worked tirelessly with colleagues to create a union, the beginning of two decades of high drama and political brinkmanship. The Teachers Guild was Shanker's organization, the New York affiliate of the American Federation of Teachers and the precursor to the modern teachers union. The Guild provided helpful information on pension rights; and later, when the board of education established a Staff Relations Plan, it provided training for members of the Staff Relations Committee, who would meet with administrators to discuss conditions in the schools.

Building the Union

The first teachers' strike in New York City was in 1959, when the evening school teachers went out. Although initiated by a rival organization, Shanker convinced his Guild colleagues to support the strike and even used his Volkswagen microbus as a coffee-mobile. The strike was successful, resulting in nearly tripled salaries for evening teachers.

Shanker soon became the first full-time field representative for the American Federation of Teachers (AFT) in New York. In 1960, with the initial merger of the Guild with a rival organization, the United Federation of Teachers (UFT) was born. In his new capacity, Shanker worked to gain official recognition for teachers and to present such serious demands as collective bargaining, duty-free lunch, dues check-off, and other standard features in contracts these past 20 years. Superintendent John J. Theobold's response was, "I don't negotiate with members of my own family." Shanker characterized this comment as the "quintessential paternalistic response."

Basically, the leadership was three men: Shanker, Charles Cogen (president of the AFT), and David Selden of the AFL-CIO, whom Shanker described as "a brilliant visionary who saw all along that when the election comes, the teachers would support the organization that supported collective bargaining." Prolonged debate ensued over whether to strike. Shanker agonized over a decision, contending with "tremendous fears that I was leading people into a terrible trap." Publicly, the union's lawyer said that the Condon-Wadlin Act was "unconstitutional," but privately he told the union leadership that no judge would support that opinion.

In the end, Shanker recommended that the union remain steadfast: "If we were to call this off, that's the end of the union. This way at least there's a chance." The strike lasted one day, and negotiations resumed. Only 5,000 teachers went out on strike, but it was enough to convince the board. Recalled Shanker, "It was a beautiful moment."

But negotiations dragged on. George Meany, President of the AFL-CIO, intervened with Mayor Wagner on behalf of the union. Scandals plagued the city, a mayoral election was approaching, and the mayor felt weakened. Reluctantly, the board and Mayor Wagner permitted a referendum to see whether teachers wanted a union. The National Education Association, the dominant teachers organization, campaigned against collective bargaining and unionism.

But the teachers voted in favor of collective bargaining by 22,000 to 8,000. "In spite of the fact that 45,000 teachers had walked through the picket lines, we managed to pull it off . . . a miracle." A labor arbitrator for the University of Wisconsin, Nathan Feinsinger, was appointed by the board to develop procedures for collective bargaining. When a second vote was held, this time to choose a bargaining agent, again the fledgling union won handily.

The first round of negotiations took place in 1962. A one-day strike ensued, but this time 22,000 teachers respected the picket lines. The upshot was "a tremendous first contract," including a duty-free lunch, a preparation period, a grievance procedure to binding arbitration, and an increase of $995 per teacher, as opposed to the usual $200 increase granted before collective bargaining.

Although the union now had a 70-page document to use as a model throughout the country, many problems lingered — not the least of which was, recalled Shanker, "the Young Turks were getting ready to try to oust Charlie Cogen from the UFT presidency" for not being militant enough. Campaigns to build a more powerful union needed to be waged in such cities as Cleveland, Philadelphia, Boston, and Detroit. Almost immediately, Cogen announced that he would retire in 1964. In a hotly contested election, Shanker was voted president. Soon the AFT won secret ballot elections in all of the cities named above.

The Radical Sixties

Although the next two contracts were negotiated without strikes, the mid-1960s witnessed a radical shift in thinking. The first school battle was over whether black power groups — led by such activists as Stokely Carmichael and H. Rap Brown — could replace a white principal from Intermediate School 201 with a black principal of their choice. They also demanded that selected teachers, white and black, be replaced. Black and white faculty members defended the white principal, as did Roy Wilkins and Whitney Young, two highly respected black leaders.

A second issue was over what to do about difficult schools, with the union calling for a More Effective Schools program: small classes, summer school, all-day kindergarten, and intensive counseling. Shanker bused his own three-year-old child to a school in Brooklyn for a pre-school program.

In 1967 a very bitter strike ensued for almost three weeks. Rhody McCoy, district superintendent in predominantly black and economically depressed Ocean Hill-Brownsville, was "a controversy waiting to erupt" into the most serious clash in the history of the New York City schools. Recalled Shanker, "McCoy gave the local draft board the names of all the people on strike." When the strike was settled, the union got an outstanding agreement, preserving More Effective Schools and class size.

Although Martin Luther King Jr. issued a statement supporting the union's education program, "almost everything in negotiations became subject to racial interpretation." Radical black activist Sonny Carson was operating in the schools, the issues of what decentralization and local control meant were festering, and the city was about to enter the Great School War.

In May 1968 Rhody McCoy sent letters of dismissal to 17 teachers "to show that he had total community control, that the union rules and the board of education tenure rules did not hold." The courts upheld the union, but racial tension was highly charged. The past three years had seen riots in several cities, including New York, and now both the Black Panthers and Sonny Carson's people were in several Brooklyn schools. When the city could not enforce the court order to reinstate the 17 teachers, the union shut down Ocean Hill-Brownsville. If the situation continued into September, the union would have "no choice but to shut the whole city down." Anti-Semitism became overt and vicious. When the Afro-American Teachers Association circulated vicious anti-Semitic material, it became a divisive issue in the union.

Perhaps this was the saddest episode in all of New York City's educational history. Shanker and McCoy debated. There were endless recriminations. "Mayor Lindsay said, 'Al, you're right,' but he couldn't figure out how to re-open the schools without setting off a race riot," Shanker remembered. "John Doar, president of the board of education, said that the union was right and the teachers would be reinstated." Ultimately, Doar told Shanker he could not re-open the schools in Ocean Hill-Brownsville because "I'm not going to have that blood on my hands." Shanker responded, "What do you think will happen at the next school, and the next school, and the one after that?" Lindsay offered to shut down any school Shanker considered unsafe if he would end the strike. In a politically astute answer, Shanker told Lindsay, "You can't live up to it. You can't give the power to close schools to the head of the teachers union."

The strike lasted until November 19, the longest in teacher history in the United States. One day Senator Javits, the senior U.S. Senator from New York, asked Shanker to take a walk with him, ostensibly to expostulate with him about a face-saving settlement on the grounds that the union had little minority support. During the walk, blacks and Hispanics approached Shanker asking for his autograph. Shanker long ago had concluded that "the black people in New York City did not want the Panthers or the Revolutionary Action Movement taking over their schools."

The strike was finally settled by the establishment of a three-person committee appointed by the state commissioner of education, which would rule on the safety of schools. Decentralization was a fact, but the union contract and board of education tenure agreements would prevail. Within a year, McCoy and his supporters "just disappeared," and the city entered a period of relative tranquillity in contract negotiations.

An Education Statesman

In 1971 Shanker was elected President of the AFT, which has its office in Washington, D.C. However, with New York City in a period of near bankruptcy, Shanker felt the membership might be demoralized if he departed to D.C. full time. So, accepting only one salary, he performed both jobs until 1986. In New York City Shanker found himself "in a new role of lending billions of dollars of pension funds to the city and negotiating give-backs." He also broadened his understanding of education by meeting regularly with the business community.

Shanker's "Where We Stand" column had begun appearing in the *New York Times* in 1970, and by 1975 it was in 60 other papers. "Where We Stand" addressed not only education initiatives and commentary, but everything from the moral fiber of the country to events in Eastern Europe. Al Shanker had begun to assume the mantle of education statesman and moral conscience of the profession. His ascendancy to the AFT presidency gave him increased national recognition.

Always active in behalf of civil rights issues, in the 1960s Shanker had marched with Martin Luther King Jr. in Alabama and Mississippi. In the late 1980s, Shanker's term on the National Endowment for Democracy — an organization that "enables business groups, trade unions, and the Democratic and Republican parties to work with like-minded groups overseas to promote democracy" — took him to Poland, Chile, Czechoslovakia, and the Philippines. During this time, he helped raise funds to overthrow the Pinochet regime in Chile, marched with Lech Walesa, and helped organize a key group that exposed Ferdinand Marcos' final election in the Philippines as fraudulent.

Shanker is an active member of such organizations as the A. Phillip Randolph Institute, the AFL-CIO Executive Committee, the Trilateral Commission, the Jewish Labor Committee, the National Academy of Education, and the National Board for Professional Standards.

Shanker's central focus, however, remains education, and his commitment to his membership is unwavering. He speaks to education and business groups dozens of times each year and is one of the most quoted education leaders in the land. He has spoken out in favor of shared decision making, national standards for testing, and serious school restructuring to improve education. Ever the tough-minded realist, Shanker told me, "In these difficult economic times, you're not going to substantially raise the salaries of 2.5 million people or significantly reduce class size. The only way to get these things is to organize schools in a different way." Shanker has promoted everything from teacher teams to the increased use of technology. He understands that teachers need a very different workplace and that students must be more fully engaged. "Historically, very few students have been able to sit still, keep quiet, and learn by listening to somebody called 'the teacher' talk to them. If you look at the General Motors Saturn Automobile plant, you see cars being produced totally differently from the way they are in traditional plants. Why not rethink the way schools operate?"

No person whose accomplishment is as large and extraordinary as is Al Shanker's works alone, but he has been the dominant force for more than 30 years in the progress of the UFT and AFT. Under his leadership, the UFT has grown from 2,500 to 110,000 members. In a very delicate series of negotiations, he was even able to organize paraprofessionals into the union. Largely black and Hispanic, "here were people who were being exploited and who could be a bridge between the teachers union and the community." This happened in 1969, one year after the Ocean Hill-Brownsville battle, and it is a particular source of pride for Shanker because he was able to help minority workers. Since Shanker became president in 1974, the AFT has more than doubled its membership to 796,000.

When I asked Shanker if he had any special hero or role model, without hesitation he named Bayard Rustin, for many years an important civil rights leader in the Afro-American community. In Shanker's words, "The great thing about Rustin was that he didn't put his finger up to see which way the wind was blowing. He had the guts to say what he felt was right no matter how unpopular it was."

Shanker's tribute to Rustin is an apt description of himself. Throughout his career, Shanker has given colleagues, friends, opponents, and great figures and dignitaries a piece of his mind, always resolutely, plainly, forthrightly.

Ernest Boyer

Ernest Boyer died at age 67 on 24 March 1997 at his home in Princeton, New Jersey, after being treated for lymphoma for nearly three years. I interviewed and had a long, pleasant lunch with Boyer in Princeton on a warm July day during the early months of his illness. He was strong and alert and never made any reference to his disease other than to concede that he was being treated for cancer in response to my, I hope, gentle question.

During our lunch in a quiet restaurant very near the university, Boyer expressed great curiosity about my background and asked me several questions about important topics in education and current events. He was, without question, one of the least self-centered, most gracious, and most courteous people I have ever interviewed.

One of Boyer's compelling interests was undergraduate education. The national report on undergraduate teaching in research universities was issued in April 1998 by the Boyer Commission, so-named to honor this very distinguished educator and person.

Formerly U.S. Commissioner of Education and Chancellor of the State University of New York, Ernest Boyer is one of the great humanists of our time. I talked with Boyer, who is now president of the Carnegie Foundation for the Advancement of Teaching, the day after he visited the Holocaust Museum in Washington, D.C., and he was still under the spell of that chilling experience. "Even 'educated' men can listen to fine music and read great literature in their homes in the evening," he said gravely, "and the next morning go to the camp to slaughter their fellow human beings."

Boyer and I spoke in his commodious office at the Carnegie Foundation, surrounded by books and photographs of himself

Originally published as "A Portrait of Ernest Boyer" in *Educational Leadership* (February 1995). Used with permission.

with such political leaders as Jimmy Carter, George Shultz, and Ronald Reagan. The Holocaust Museum remained with Boyer as we began to speak of education and his career. "Many of those perpetrators of ultimate evil held advanced degrees," commented Boyer, "so the questions that came to me once again are those I've asked for 40 years: What are the most essential aims of education? What is the relationship between education and ethical behavior? Are we, in fact, educating toward evil if we fail to place knowledge in a larger moral context?"

Early Lessons, Compelling Questions

Throughout his career, Boyer has always raised large questions, pondering such issues as aesthetics, ethics, and the environment as he thought about curriculum or political change. The bedrock of Boyer's humanism is an intense engagement with people.

Born in Dayton, Ohio, one year before the onset of the Depression, Boyer witnessed the privation of that era but was fortunate to escape its personal touch. Ernie, his mother, and two brothers worked in the family greeting card and office supplies mail-order business. From his father, a successful businessman, he learned "lessons of persistence and diligence and hard work," but it was his paternal grandfather, William H. Boyer, a minister, who directed him toward "a people-centered life." He admired his grandfather's compassion, especially toward children, as well as his ability to listen and to ask good questions.

Throughout his schooling, Boyer was consistently drawn to teachers who emphasized language and the exhilaration of learning. Miss Rice, his first-grade teacher, kindled Ernie's interest in language and writing. Later, a high school history teacher, Carlton Wittlinger, showed young Boyer that "history was not frozen but in the making," Boyer said. Wittlinger also told Ernie that he could be a good student, an affirmation that helped Boyer rethink who he was and where he was going.

Boyer took his newfound confidence to Greenville College, a small liberal arts school in Illinois, where he became engaged in debate and college politics. Debate, said Boyer, inspired his "interest in the whole field of language. . . and taught me how to manage ideas and words." In addition, his election as president of the student body at Greenville, an affirmation by his peers, had a profound influence on Boyer, who had never before thought of himself as a leader.

In graduate school, literature and speech dominated Boyer's interests, ultimately leading to a doctorate in speech pathology from the University of Southern California and a postdoctoral fellowship in medical audiology at the University of Iowa Hospital. Boyer's view of language as "an interactive reverberating system," though always fascinating to him, soon ceased to be the central focus in his career.

After teaching at Loyola University in Los Angeles, Boyer became academic dean at Upland College. From then on, his commitment was to education administration. At Upland, he introduced a program where the mid-year term — the month of January — became a creative study time. This 4-1-4 plan has been emulated by hundreds of other colleges. Boyer held two more administrative posts in California. At the first, which was sponsored by the Western College Association, he focused on the question, "What does it mean to be an educated teacher?" The goal of the second, at the University of California-Santa Barbara, was "to connect the university with surrounding schools."

A Time of Growth

In 1965, Boyer headed east to become executive dean at the State University of New York. He remained at SUNY until 1977, seven years as its chancellor. Reflecting on those years, Boyer remarked, "New York is a great place to work. The politicians play hardball, but they know the rules, and Rockefeller was one of the most remarkable public figures I've known."

This period was one of enormous growth in the SUNY system and also a time when Boyer generated one new idea after another. For example, he established Empire State College, a noncampus college where adults studied with mentors through contracts. "The system is still in place," added Boyer, "and all the data show that it works at least as well as traditional education." The concept institutionalized the notion of flexible, lifelong learning and gave it credibility. In addition, Boyer launched an experimental, three-year Bachelor of Arts program in response to a question he had often pondered, "Why four years and not three or five?"

Another approach Boyer took to personalize the huge SUNY institution was to reach out to faculty and administrators. The summer institutes and retreats he initiated were on a human scale and served as seedbeds for ideas. From establishing a five-year review of presidents, to creating the new rank of Distinguished Teaching Professor, to approving statewide student government — the ideas kept coming.

Boyer also had an enduring interest in international education. In 1976, SUNY signed the first agreement between the Soviet Union and the United States for undergraduate exchanges. SUNY also signed a similar agreement with universities in Israel. "My goal as chancellor," Boyer said, "was to emphasize the human side of organizations, the creative side, the international side of organizations."

The Move to Washington

In 1977, President Carter invited Boyer to become the 23rd Commissioner of Education. At first, Boyer resisted the Washington job offer, partly because at that time the education office was buried in the Department of Health, Education and Welfare, and partly because the bloom was not off the New York job. Ultimately, he found the Washington experience to be invaluable. As he expressed it, "I became informed about the issues of public education, got involved in discussions about excellence and equality, and confronted more directly the crisis that may overwhelm us in the end: the gap between the haves and the have-nots."

One of Boyer's first tasks was to redirect the discussion about equity. His predecessors in the 1960s and early 1970s had focused on equality of opportunity, a long-overdue issue that Boyer wanted to reintroduce. Boyer was the first commissioner to implement the new Education for All Handicapped Act, and he became acutely aware of the plight of Native Americans. As commissioner, he redirected effort and funds to this group that had historically been "so scandalously neglected."

Boyer found Washington to be more challenging than New York, but he managed to secure federal funds for education — cumulatively receiving a 40% increase in three years. He also created the Horace Mann Learning Center in the U.S. Office of Education to promote lifelong learning — and miraculously it lasted 10 years. That program was the exception, however; Boyer found that "federal agencies don't have continuity of leadership." Permanent job holders were reluctant to pledge loyalty to any idea or leader because it or the person would soon be replaced.

Boyer did all that he could, therefore, to focus on the largest idea he believed the federal government was duty-bound to pursue, morally and constitutionally: to bridge the gap between the haves and have-nots and to overcome the handicaps that come out of economic disadvantage and social prejudice. Toward the end of the Carter Administration, Boyer received an offer from the Carnegie Foundation for the Advancement of Teaching, and he left Washington for a career that mixed contemplation with activism.

"The Best Education Job in the Country"

The Carnegie Foundation was formally chartered by Congress in 1906. The currency of the foundation is words based on ideas, irresistible to Boyer, who had been a member of the Carnegie board of trustees. Over a period of decades, through dozens of reports, books, and seminars, the foundation had built deep credibility in the education community: "When the foundation reports are released, people take notice," said Boyer. Now in his 13th year at Carnegie, Boyer is certain he made the right move: "It's the best education job in the country. . . . I work on ideas I think are consequential and try to shape the debate. . . . I am in an organization that is 90% ideas and 10% hassle."

One of the first things Boyer did was to broaden the foundation agenda to include the public schools. In 1980, he asked the board to launch a study of the American high school. In initiating his first proposal, Boyer cautioned the board, "You can't have good colleges if you don't have good schools." The result was the highly influential *High School* (1983) completed just before the release of *A Nation at Risk*. The book insisted that teachers be at the vortex of any reform and called for community service — a new Carnegie unit that would give young people purpose beyond self-satisfaction. Community service was a concept not mentioned in *A Nation at Risk*.

College: The Undergraduate Experience followed logically in 1986. This book emphasized excellence in undergraduate college teaching, as well as attention to social and co-curricular experiences, which are so important during the years between adolescence and adulthood. "The attention that's been given in the last five years to undergraduate education and to good teaching have been strongly stirred by the priorities we have been pushing here," said Boyer.

In 1991, *Scholarship Reconsidered,* a report that has received more response than Boyer ever imagined, set priorities for a college faculty, which include discovering knowledge through research and then integrating and applying that knowledge in useful ways. *Scholarship Reconsidered* will soon be followed by *Scholarship Assessed,* which will evaluate the role of the faculty.

Boyer's resolve — through the debates, speeches, and reports of the past 10 years — has been to shine a beacon on undergraduate education and, as he put it, especially to inspire faculty to recommit themselves to teaching. A recent report, *Ready to Learn,* describes how the nation can respond to that education goal.

The Big Picture

A conversation with Ernest Boyer moves recursively among the importance of the humanities, the centrality of language, the need for larger purpose, the role of a nonsectarian spiritual element in education, and the foundation of his life: his wife and four children. About his wife, Kathryn, he says, "I have drawn more inspiration from my wife of 43 years than any other person on the planet." His children are all involved in varied careers of service. One son is a chaplain, his daughter followed his wife's career in nursing, and two sons are involved in cross-cultural education — one in Belize, who works with Mayans, and the other in Maryland, who edits a journal on American Indian education.

Ernest Boyer's achievements and influence are vast. He holds honorary degrees from 123 colleges and universities; was designated Educator of the Year in 1990 by *U.S. News and World Report;* was named to national commissions by Presidents Carter, Nixon, and Ford; is a member of the Board of Directors of Lincoln Center; and was a recent recipient of one of the Charles Frankel Prizes for humanities presented by President Clinton — to name just a few honors and achievements. But it is his clear-sighted humanistic view of education in an era when science, math, and testing have been in ascendance that makes him a treasured spokesperson for the spiritual and human center of the great education enterprise. For 40 years, Ernest Boyer has been resolute about what matters. As he expressed it:

> To increase test scores or to be world class in math and science without empowering students or affirming the dignity of human life is to lose the essence of what we and education are presumably all about. . . .
>
> In the end, our goal must be not only to prepare students for careers, but also to enable them to live with dignity and purpose; not only to give knowledge to the student, but also to channel knowledge to humane ends. . . . Educating a new generation of Americans to their full potential is still our most compelling obligation.

Photograph by Diane Bondareff. Courtesy of the Office of the Mayor, City of New York.

Rudolph Giuliani

*When I interviewed Mayor Giuliani in 1995, he had just com-
pleted making Chancellor Ramon Cortines uncomfortable enough
to leave his position as the head of the New York City school system and was using my and others' articles to state his terms for a
new chancellor. Soon after, Chancellor Rudy Crew was hired. For
nearly three years the relationship between Giuliani and Crew
was very good, but in the spring of 1999 it foundered on the issues
of vouchers and school construction. Crew's contract was not
renewed by the board of education in December 1999. After re-
sisting the appointment of Harold O. Levy, the interim chancellor,
the mayor finally relented in May 2000 and now is working with
his third chancellor in seven years.*

*For a few months in early 2000, Giuliani pursued the Senate
seat that also was sought by Hillary Clinton, but he dropped out
of the race in May 2000 after learning that he had prostate cancer and that his marriage, in difficulty for years, was unraveling.
His future after he leaves the mayor's office in a year (there is a
two-term limit) is now unclear.*

*I was impressed by the fact that the mayor could respond to
some 25 questions, several in great detail, during our interview
without once using the thick black loose-leaf notebook on education held by his communications director, Chrystyne Lategano,
and offered to him at the beginning of the interview. The mayor
answered question after question on test scores, the number and
types of schools in the huge city system, and issues that had come
up during his first year in office without the least hesitation. After
the interview, when I checked many of the answers, I found that
Giuliani had been unerringly accurate.*

Originally published as "Education in New York City: An Interview
with Mayor Rudolph Giuliani" in *Phi Delta Kappan* (December 1995).
Used with permission.

Rudolph Giuliani is angry about the way education works in New York City, and he wants everyone to know it. When he talks about the education system in the city, he uses such words and phrases as "dead," "useless bureaucrats," and "rigor mortis." New York's 107th mayor is absolutely convinced that failure is inherent in the current system and that the system must undergo dramatic change. The bureaucrats at 110 Livingston Street (school headquarters), Mayor Giuliani says, "perpetuate themselves. The things they are doing are largely useless, and then those things are superimposed on the people who are useful, and it kills their creativity and their morale."

There are approximately 1.1 million students in the city's 1,085 schools. Many of the schools are old and in serious disrepair. In 1994 the graduation rate after four years of high school was an abysmal 44.3%. That same year, more than half of the city's children scored below grade level in reading, and almost half scored below grade level in math. The dropout rate for all students stands at 18.7%, and the budget is "inscrutable — it is virtually impossible to tell how much is spent on administrators, bureaucrats, vendors, contractors of all types, and programs imposed by Washington, Albany, and the courts," Mayor Giuliani says. Add to that the pervasive corruption in several local school boards, and you have a prescription for continual failure.

The system the mayor sees in New York is very far from the one he remembers. Rudy Giuliani grew up in a working-class family of small shopkeepers. His first teacher was his mother. She "began teaching me to read when I was about 3½ or 4 years old," he recalls. "She spent a lot of time getting me interested in learning, particularly history. She knew how to tell a story and make you want to read."

As a youngster, Giuliani went to parochial elementary and secondary schools, graduating from Bishop Loughlin High School in Brooklyn in 1961. He received his undergraduate degree from Manhattan College in 1965 and has clear memories of good teaching at all the schools he attended. He recalls such outstanding teachers as Brother Kevin in high school and Brother Alexander Joseph at Manhattan College, both Christian Brothers who took extra time with students and who were "tough, demanding, and exacting" on their students and on themselves.

The memory of that parochial school education is important enough to the mayor that today he holds up the Catholic school system as a possible model for the city's public schools. In a speech this past August at the Wharton Club, Giuliani referred to his alma mater, Bishop Loughlin High School, and pointed out that its principal, Brother James Bonilla, can set education priorities and spending policies "right at the school level." Giuliani went on to recommend that the parochial schools — in which there are high standards, school-based management, and school-based budgeting — could serve as a template for the city's crumbling system. He noted that the parochial schools have 151,000 students in New York City but have very few bureaucrats in their hierarchy.

Giuliani loved every minute at New York University School of Law. Many of his classmates saw the study of law as necessary to get where they wanted to go, but Giuliani was attracted powerfully and immediately to the law itself. A teacher who made a great impression on him was Professor Childress, who taught contracts and introduced Giuliani to the Socratic method. In Childress' classes Giuliani had to think, not just absorb information. Another teacher whose memory has stayed with the mayor was Irving Younger, who taught evidence and gave him his "first sense of wanting to be a trial lawyer, most particularly in the U.S. attorney's office."

After law school, Giuliani clerked for two years with federal judge Lloyd McMahon, "a natural teacher." Under his tutelage, the young attorney began to understand that "good leadership and going against the bureaucracy" led to success.

Prior to being elected mayor, Rudy Giuliani was best known as a crime fighter, a terrific prosecutor, and a cross-examiner who, as the U.S. attorney for the southern district of New York, took on both organized crime figures and white-collar criminals from Wall Street — and frequently won. As mayor, Giuliani's first priority was to stabilize the city "and create a sense of safety and security." In the past 18 months, by virtually any standard, the mayor and his police commissioner, William Bratton, have substantially reduced everything from the murder rate to the rate of car theft. They have done so by acting aggressively, going against accepted procedure and belief, and turning responsibility back to precinct commanders, making them accountable for improvement in their geographic areas. In many ways, the police department has become the gold standard for progress in the city — a department to which the school system is frequently compared and found wanting.

There are, of course, some pockets of excellence in the city school system. Several of the magnet schools and specialized high schools — Bronx High School of Science and Stuyvesant High School spring immediately to mind — have long histories of excellence with academically talented students. In the past 15 years, principal Deborah Meier, the MacArthur fellow who is now coordinator of New York's Annenberg grant, and her band of creative principals and teachers have developed several fine elementary schools and a high school in East Harlem. That program is being expanded with the Annenberg grant money, but only a tiny percentage of New York City children will be affected. Essentially, Meier and her colleagues have created many very small schools that reach out in personal ways to students and emphasize high academic standards. The children in these schools in East Harlem are among the most disadvantaged in the city. However, they want to be in these schools, their parents want them to be there, the parents have been drawn into the life of the schools, and the staff members want to work in these schools.

"The whole movement toward choice in East Harlem that now goes back at least 10 or 12 years is a remarkable example of success by people who are willing not to follow the rules," Mayor Giuliani says. "It's also a remarkable example of what's wrong with the board of education. It happened against all of their rules, all of their teaching, all of their thinking. And it succeeded really well and has become a national model. But you can't spread it because the board of education is afraid of it." To create the East Harlem schools, it took a group of dedicated, rule-resisting administrators and teachers — rogue educators by city standards. The mayor acknowledges that each school in the city is different and must find its own way, just as the people in East Harlem did. "If you're in a situation where you have a school that has tremendous and difficult stresses in it, you're not going to solve that school's problems by following a priori rules that are laid down for some other situation."

While the symptoms of failure are clear to the mayor, and he is not lacking for solutions to the schools' problems, he is frustrated by his lack of political power to effect change in the huge and cumbersome system. "I don't select the chancellor. I hand him the money, but I can't tell him how to use it." In New York City, the mayor gets to appoint two of the seven members of the board of education. Each of the five borough presidents gets to appoint one board member, and rarely is there enough political harmony to have a board that is responsive to the mayor. Once appointed, the board is completely independent of the mayor.

Mayor Giuliani favors a system like the one recently legislated in Chicago, in which the mayor selects a commissioner of education. He wants a system in which the mayor and the commissioner have "a shared philosophy, a shared direction," and have to answer to the people who elected the mayor.

The commissioner system has worked well in the police department, and the mayor frequently cites examples of how he and the police commissioner have reduced crime in the city and how the schools could benefit from a similar arrangement. In fact, crime is a serious problem in the city's schools, and the mayor claims that it is not being addressed. "You've got situations in this city where schools are more dangerous than other parts of the neighborhood," he notes. The school system has its own security force, which has recently been plagued by scandals and is not very effective, according to the mayor. "There is no academic program attractive enough that it is going to get a parent to say, 'I'm going to put my child in danger. I'm going to put my child in a school in which children get knifed, teachers get beaten, or some children have to be given money to pay other children to protect them'." The mayor sees this state of affairs as symptomatic of the problems of the school system. When he offered to have the police department take over school security, the response from the chancellor and the board was, basically, "We'll do nothing different."

When asked what, exactly, he would like the new chancellor to do, the mayor is very clear. First, the chancellor will have to delegate authority to excellent people. "You need to know how to select people and how to be demanding of what they have to accomplish. You have to have a very clear vision of how you're going to change the system, and you have to articulate it and stick to it and be willing to be measured by whether or not you succeed in getting there." Lack of accountability, in Giuliani's view, is a major defect in the present system. The mayor has said on many occasions that, while there are several measures by which his administration can be gauged in the next election, voters should "not vote for me based on the schools. I don't control them. . . . The chancellor is not accountable either. The system is designed to remove accountability."

The next two items on the mayor's agenda for education are money and safety. He is convinced that, until the schools are an oasis of physical safety and the system's budget is turned upside down so that the schools get what they need first, there is little hope for improving the academic program. Physical safety can be handled by the police, "but the chancellor, who is independent, has to be willing to allow that." In a revised budget system, each school would work with "a vastly shrunk bureaucracy" to determine what that school needs in order to operate effectively. In a school-based budget, funds would go first to each of the city's schools, and then the central bureaucracy, lean and effective, would get the much-reduced amount it needs to coordinate necessary services and to ensure accountability.

Academic standards could then be the central focus of each school's efforts, and they would be "raised substantially." The mayor's notion is that each school should be given the resources and the support it needs to improve its educational program. The principal would be held accountable; and if she or he did not do the job, there would be a process to handle that situation, including the power to remove people who cannot work effectively. "The standards should be fairly obvious, and they should be clear. And they should not be so burdensome that they remove creativity," Giuliani says. I ask the mayor what role the local boards would play and volunteer that, from what he has said, it sounds as if the local boards should be removed. His answer: "That's a good idea. That's a really good idea. . . . The principals, the teachers, the parents, and the students will make the schools work."

Accountability is never a bad word in Mayor Giuliani's vocabulary, but it can be a bad word for a leader who is incompetent. "The last thing an incompetent principal wants is to be accountable," Giuliani says. "Somebody who really wants to do the job wants to be accountable. He wants to prove himself." Mayor Giuliani wants to be judged by the progress he has made toward solving the problem of crime, improving the quality of life in the city, and meeting other goals articulated in his campaign for mayor. This is what he believes any leader should want, but a baseline from which to measure progress or the lack of it is necessary. "We aren't even at the first stage yet. The first stage is to have accurate statistics," he points out. But the schools, he claims, have done a fine job of hiding or obfuscating the statistics. The mayor sees the issue of standards and baseline achievement data in clear, stark terms.

"We have schools to educate youngsters; to teach them to read, write, add, and subtract; and to prepare them for the next level of education or for taking up their responsibilities as citizens. Let's measure schools according to each school's baseline and whether or not the school is improving or regressing in the basic things that schools are supposed to do," Giuliani argues. "Give them the resources to get the job done; give them the support to get the job done. The commissioner or chancellor has to have the authority to remove the ones that are failing, to put a new principal and a new leadership team into schools in which the test scores are declining."

Support for the schools in New York City is in serious decline, Mayor Giuliani fears. He believes that parents will insist on a system that allows them to determine how their children are educated. The mayor says firmly, "I don't support a voucher system, but I see the political support for it building." He places the blame for this squarely on the board of education, which is unresponsive to any meaningful change, even when "the system is failing."

One example the mayor provides of board recalcitrance is his suggestion that the board look at the possibility of hiring a new chancellor from the business community, someone who could take a fresh look at the school system and all of the assumptions on which it is based. "Their reaction was like the octopus that's caught and shoots out all the ink — an amazing overreaction. I didn't say they had to choose a business leader. I said to them, *'Consider* a business leader.' Just think of the anti-intellectual attitude, the bureaucratic inertia, the inability to display even a tiny flexibility of thought that their 'no' conveys."

The New York City school system is spending more than $8 billion a year, and, except in a few instances that are rarely replicated, it is not succeeding. The mayor is determined to do what he can to return power to the individual schools and to remove the layers of bureaucracy. He knows that schools will make individual choices about how to proceed, but he finds that liberating. "Give a school a chance to succeed, and it's probably going to make different choices than another school somewhere else. Bureaucracies hate that. Bureaucracies hate differences."

When the mayor was in the U.S. Justice Department, he lectured FBI agents on how to solve major, sophisticated crimes. He told the agents that, if they followed the many rules of the FBI slavishly, "the only crimes you'll ever solve are those crimes committed by the rules. You'll solve none of the sophisticated crimes, none of the creative crimes, none of the unusual ones."

In the end, Mayor Giuliani says somewhat wistfully, the issue is not between him and the board or between him and the chancellor. "Education does not take place at 110 Livingston Street. It takes place in 1,085 schools," he says. It is there that the resources and the accountability must be placed, or nothing will happen. The bureaucrats want to focus on bus contracts and contracts for pencils and plumbing. But it's not about that either. "It isn't about budget fights with city hall or Albany or Washington. What it's about are the 1,085 schools," he concludes. "If the people in the schools can't make them work, there's nothing the central bureaucracy can do for them."

Photograph by John Foraste. Courtesy of Brown University.

Theodore Sizer

I published two articles on Ted Sizer, the first in Educational Leadership *in 1993 and the second in the* Phi Delta Kappan *in 1996. Sizer is a very thoughtful, professorial man. His responses to questions are measured and articulate, never any sense of hurry or scatter to his answers.*

Ted Sizer wears the tasteful, donnish clothes you would expect of a man who has spent most of his career at Harvard, Phillips Academy, and Brown University. This is a man who has spent a lot of time visiting public schools and talking to teachers and administrators but has not personally broken up many student fights in the corridor or worried about the bus schedule, though he and his wife served as co-principals of a small charter school in 1998-1999.

Interestingly and sensibly, two of the people Sizer chose to work with him at Brown on the Annenberg Challenge were gritty, experienced, and extremely successful public school principals, Dennis Littky and Deborah Meier, both of whom I have interviewed for articles. Littky is at least a decade younger than Sizer, often dresses like a hourly worker in spite of his middle-class background and Ph.D. from the University of Michigan, and has an extremely quick and creative intelligence. Deborah Meier is slightly older than Sizer, comes from a cultured, leftist, New York background, and is somewhat less rapid-fire than Littky but more reflective. Both Littky and Meier care deeply about kids and schools and respect Sizer enormously, a respect that Ted Sizer returns at least in equal measure.

About half a mile south of Brown University, Ted Sizer's modest brick-walled office sits at the end of the first floor of a converted industrial building, 200 feet from the Providence River

---

Originally published as "Here for the Long Haul: An Interview with Theodore Sizer" in *Phi Delta Kappan* (June 1996). Used with permission.

that bisects Rhode Island's capital city. The Coalition of Essential Schools and the many projects of the Annenberg Institute occupy two floors of the building — a total of 13,000 square feet — and are beginning to spread to a third floor. Sizer's work has increased in scope and complexity in the past three years with the growth of the Coalition and the addition of the Annenberg Institute. I ask him about how he handles the administration of so many responsibilities.

In reply he is generous with praise for his colleagues, emphasizing that he's less important than he once was in this evolving and growing reform enterprise. "It's a chorus of voices now, not just my voice," he says. He singles out for praise such people as Vartan Gregorian, the president of Brown University, which is host to both the coalition and the institute; several long-time colleagues, such as Paula Evans, Robert McCarthy, and Joseph McDonald; and Dennis Littky, Deborah Meier, and Howard Fuller, who serve as senior fellows in the institute.

But it is clear to any visitor who wanders through the offices and talks to people that Ted Sizer is the instigator, guiding spirit, and intellectual center of the building's activities. Sizer himself understands that "the 900-pound gorilla in this building is the Coalition of Essential Schools, and it was on the reputation of the coalition that the Annenberg Institute was launched by its donors." Sizer is the founder and chairman of the coalition, as well as the founding director of the Annenberg Institute. He's also the person who meets with the senior staff members working on various projects, and he's the person with the global view of the many reform activities that emanate from this building. The notion that there is no template or model for American schools — just guiding principles and a deep respect for the culture of an individual school — informs all the work of the coalition and the institute. And that vision is vintage Ted Sizer.

When Sizer graduated from Yale in 1953, like most young men of his generation he entered the military. He calls his two years as an artillery officer "a very influential experience for a young man." Many of the 17- and 18-year-old boys who served in his unit were school dropouts, but they performed their duties perfectly well. "Whatever troops you got had to deliver. If one person didn't do it, he put everybody's life at stake. That made a deep impression. There was no tracking in the army, just the beliefs that somehow these young men had to be trained and had to be reliable and that all soldiers can learn," he recalls.

After the army, a year of teaching at Roxbury Latin School, and a year of graduate school, Sizer and his new wife went off to Australia, where he taught history and geography at the Melbourne Grammar School for boys. With an M.A.T. (master of arts in teaching) in social studies from Harvard and a year of classroom experience, Sizer believed he knew something about what constituted good pedagogy and expected to try his ideas in Melbourne.

The school in Australia was very traditional and, in fact, had a strong military program. The boys were organized into the Australian equivalent of ROTC, so that "the entire school constituted a fully equipped infantry battalion." On spring vacation, the boys went on maneuvers. Sizer came to understand that much of a generation of men had been wiped out in World War II, that Australians "were deeply afraid of the likely renewed assault from Asian powers," and that these boys were expected to serve and did so gladly. "The shock for me," he recalls, "was that much of what my teacher training said should not work, worked just fine. That's when I learned the importance of culture. You cannot say *always* or *never* except at the extremes. You have to be very sensitive to who the families are, what the community is, what the expectations are." In 1959 Sizer returned to Harvard to work on a doctorate.

In 1964, after a short period as an assistant professor at Harvard and director of its M.A.T. program, Sizer became the dean of Harvard's Graduate School of Education at age 31 and remained in that post for nearly eight years. These were heady times, encompassing everything from the tremendous infusion of money into education during the Johnson Administration to the difficult and even violent Vietnam War protests. Daniel Patrick Moynihan and Christopher Jencks were faculty members; so were Nathan Glazer and Lawrence Kohlberg. Carol Gilligan was a graduate student. The intellectual ferment was as passionate as anything a young dean could want. Sizer was particularly influenced by two seminars: the Equal Educational Opportunity Seminar and the seminar run at the Center for Studies in Education and Development. They called everything into question and shone a very bright light onto issues. "Being part of that intense conversation was absolutely extraordinary because it pushed every corner of the system."

By late 1971 Sizer was exhausted and wanted to do something different, something that would bring him much closer to adolescents. He considered undergraduate college teaching, but he was drawn to work in a high school. When the offer came to be the headmaster at Phillips Academy in Andover, Massachusetts, he decided it was too grand an opportunity to miss. There are, of course, many students at Andover who come from prominent families and are extremely well prepared for the work at this demanding school. However, there are also students who are at Andover on scholarship because their families have little or no money. These students want to do the work but may have been "miserably schooled" before arriving at the school. Andover is well endowed and has a commitment to work with all students, so "we clothed these kids, we fed them, we fixed their teeth, we flew their mothers in to visit them. We did not look at their age or what they had covered in their previous schools, only at their performance."

Every incoming student at Andover enters an English competence course and stays there, without prejudice, until he or she can read and write well enough to do the work. The entire school was driven by performance and students' needs. "The ultimate objective was the diploma, which had a common standard," but the diploma might be conferred at age 16 or 19, whenever the student performed well enough to deserve it — but always without prejudice. Watching the difference such choice made was very instructive for Sizer. By and large, all the students at Andover wanted to be there, and that "changed the nature of the relationship" between the students and teachers. Universal student achievement was no longer a theory but something Sizer saw operating every day. It was hard, it took effort on everyone's part, and there were failures. But it could be done. "Schools make a difference, but you've got to focus. You can change people's lives."

In 1981 Sizer left Andover to chair a large research project called A Study of High Schools. Out of that experience came *Horace's Compromise* and the beginnings of the coalition. Sizer had become convinced that every student could perform well if given the proper setting and support, that no two schools would be alike because no two school cultures were alike, and that shining the powerful light of intellectual inquiry on complex problems could lead to new questions and possible solutions. The coalition started at Brown University in 1984 as a very small effort to work with five or 10 schools that would operate around a set of Nine Common Principles, including: the purpose of school is to help students think; exhibitions are superior to tests because they help you and the student see what the youngster really knows; you teach best when you know your students well, so no secondary teacher should see more than 80 students each day; and students learn best when they believe what they are learning is important.

The Nine Common Principles have not changed over the 12 years of their application, but the quotidian efforts of the coalition have shifted many times. For one thing, the coalition now includes 940 schools in 37 states and two foreign countries. These schools are public and private, wealthy and poor. Most are secondary schools, though more elementary schools join each year. At least one-third of the students in coalition schools are from minority groups. There is also considerably more emphasis on giving families and students a choice about where to go to school. Wealthy people have always had such a choice and have exercised it. They could send their children to a private school, or they could move to a community with good public schools. Moreover, they could benefit from the tax laws when they purchased a home.

People like Anthony Alvarado and Deborah Meier have demonstrated that choice can work in the public schools of East Harlem, New York. "It changes the nature of the contract" by putting children in a school where they want to be and where they are wanted, but doing so requires "totally open access." If a school gets very popular, you do not make it bigger. You open a similar school to give parents a nearly parallel choice. If a school fails, you close it. "Under the present system," Sizer argues, "demonstrably incompetent schools have no incentive to improve." But you can have several small schools inside a single building, and you can dissolve an individual school and start a new one on the same site. You are doing nothing for children, however, if you continue to support schools that consistently fail. Schools should enroll no more than a few hundred students, and the ratio of staff to students must allow for a high degree of personalization.

Today, the coalition is supporting clusters of small schools to help offer choice. Sizer argues that no one really knows what a school district is. We call New York City a single district; we also call Ansley, Nebraska, one. "There are a lot of parents who are respectful of their local schools but really want something different." The number of students being schooled at home or in private, charter, magnet, or other settings is growing. The laws, directives, board policies, superintendents, and governors change so frequently that "you don't know which way to go. It's in that kind of chaos that sensible people say, 'The current system isn't working'."

I questioned Sizer about single-issue schools or extreme schools developing out of choice for all students. "I believe the American people are smarter than that," he replied. "In a system of choice and in a system of very bright lights where every school is portrayed publicly — students' real work and real evidence — the people will decide. Vicious schools and utterly incompetent schools will be exposed."

When a new school phones the coalition, the first effort is to put that school in touch with a nearby school with successful coalition experience or with a coalition regional center. As the coalition has grown, this has become the way to get help to people without directing every effort from Providence. However, under the aegis of the coalition and the Annenberg Institute, a great deal is happening in Providence that can benefit schools. Schools undergoing reform need as much help and support as they can get. Ted Sizer well understands that "it's exceedingly difficult to change schools — and particularly in a volatile environment where assessment systems, political control, and collective bargaining are themselves in flux." He also concedes that the coalition might work in a significant and lasting way for 20% of the schools that sign on. The wisest course is to have schools in clusters helping one another, while back in Providence work and training continue for all the schools to draw on as they wish.

For most schools that do not succeed, the missing ingredient is sustained support from every level of governance and from every constituency involved with the school. In Providence, considerable work is under way to supply ideas, materials, and expertise to support schools at every level. The Providence reform efforts are still inchoate and subject to change. Basically, the enterprises are organized around three somewhat interdependent divisions: the Coalition of Essential Schools, the Annenberg Institute, and the Annenberg Challenge. In addition, from time to time, special projects are incubated in Providence that don't fit neatly under any rubric. All efforts lead to Sizer's office, though President Gregorian or some other staff member may play a central role in any given project.

A main focus in Providence is professional development, to "put as much backbone as we can into helping schools." Training programs emphasize listening and respecting the local culture. The National School Reform Faculty "now has several hundred veteran school people who are trained and experienced in helping other schools," Sizer says. The 50 Schools Project reinforces the notion of clusters. There is a cluster in Chicago, another that runs through upstate New York and parts of New Hampshire and Maine, and a third that extends from Jefferson City, Kentucky, to Cincinnati. The Annenberg Challenge is an effort to put together groups of schools, philanthropists, reformers, and others to form nonprofit entities devoted to increasing the quality of learning and improving the daily reality of public education. President

Gregorian spearheads this effort and is the principal advisor working to make Ambassador Annenberg's stunning 1993 grant of $500 million develop the kind of synergy of money and people required to bring about substantial and durable reform. President Gregorian is "emotionally committed" to this enterprise and works extremely closely with Ted Sizer.

The coalition's fall forum is the annual gathering of people interested in school reform, in the work of the coalition, and in what the Annenberg Institute is doing. This year 3,700 people attended the meeting in New York City and exchanged information about how to do the work of school reform. The extraordinary attendance in an expensive locale was heartening to Sizer. "The very large number of people who care about things I care about is very, very precious — overwhelming." Deborah Meier's work in New York — perhaps the most complete example of how what is "precious" to Sizer can work — continues and is expanding under the Annenberg Challenge. Now working with both elementary and high school students in East Harlem, Meier and her colleagues are demonstrating that everything — quality of student work, college acceptance, parental satisfaction, and daily attendance — improves in a system of small schools of choice with high standards and dedicated staff members operating in the context of the coalition's guiding principles.

The coalition is a partner in the ATLAS Communities Project, a joint effort that includes Howard Gardner's work at Harvard, James Comer's work at Yale, and the work of the Educational Development Center in Cambridge, Massachusetts. Dennis Littky is working on the Rhode Island Project, which includes the design of a new school that will emphasize career and academic work and resonate with ideas for other educational designs throughout the country.

Various research projects are coming out of the Annenberg Institute. "A major project is the School Change Study, headed by Patricia Wasley. This is a team of people who have watched and recorded very carefully how change took place in six schools across the country," Sizer says. The Exhibitions Project is developing "a collection of all kinds of exhibitions, so you can sit down and see a wide variety of work." There is also a Digital Portfolio Project that "is a shift from one-shot exhibitions to a portfolio [built] on the platform of a computer." This will make large amounts of information available to teachers, including examples of how students defend their work.

Arguably, the combined efforts of the coalition and the Annenberg Institute and Challenge are the largest and most significant attempt at school reform in the history of American education. Through newsletters, pamphlets, telephones, and e-mail, an enormous amount of information is promulgated each month. Such efforts as the schools in East Harlem or the high school completely revitalized by Dennis Littky and his staff in Winchester, New Hampshire, are unquestioned successes.

But the coalition also has its detractors among people who want a specific plan to guide them. "We are deliberately respectful of local culture and local authority," Sizer states, "and we endlessly get criticized for that: What's your model to implement? The word *implement* is the wrong word. We're asking people to think differently about learning and children."

The work of the coalition and of the institute is "messy," and Sizer is enormously grateful that Brown University has an entrepreneurial spirit and that both Howard Swearer, the former president, and President Gregorian have proved themselves to be champions of subtle, sophisticated, and risk-taking ventures. "The kind of work we do doesn't have the precision respected by traditional education people, and I don't think it can by its nature," says Sizer. He well understands what he's up against. But there is a refreshingly ingenuous quality in this bright, determined man that makes his enterprises work. He's under no illusion that anything will happen quickly or that the work will be easy. But in the end he is tenaciously confident and says buoyantly, "So it's slow business, and we're here for the long haul."

Stephen Jay Gould

Stephen Jay Gould was the most difficult person I interviewed. He and his wife graciously invited me into their loft home in New York's Greenwich Village. Both before and after the interview, the Goulds showed me what they had done to make their commodious loft quite a beautiful and tasteful place, a place where he could write and think and his wife could do her art.

The interview itself was challenging because Gould did not respond to the opportunity to speak freely or expansively — unless and until I posed a very specific question. Questions such as "Tell me about your Brooklyn childhood?" or "What was it like to be a student in the New York City schools in the late 1940s and early 1950s?" were followed rapidly by the admonition, "Be much more specific!"

Once I adapted precisely to what Gould wanted, specificity such as "Tell me about the three teachers to whom you dedicated your book, The Panda's Thumb. *Talk about what, exactly, made them teachers you regard as excellent and memorable," Stephen Jay Gould became a wonderful interviewee. He needed, demanded, a very specific prompt, and then he became free and expansive, almost always supplying considerable information far afield from the original prompt.*

Strictly speaking, Stephen Jay Gould is not an educator. He's a paleontologist, Harvard professor, and arguably America's finest and most commercially successful serious science writer. He does not profess to know what is laudable or lamentable about the public schools, since his career in education has been devoted to highly motivated graduate students and undergraduates. Indeed, he describes Harvard as "a school of valedictorians — highly

Originally published as "Joltin' Joe and the Pursuit of Excellence: An Interview with Stephen Jay Gould" in *Phi Delta Kappan* (January 1997). Used with permission.

skilled and pretty well motivated" and hardly an accurate micro-cosm of America's youth. However, Gould does have very strong feelings about what he valued in his own education and what he values in the education world he knows — not to mention what he misses in today's students and in American culture.

I interviewed Professor Gould in his modern, beautifully reno-vated, spacious New York loft, which is filled with his artist wife's colorful and fascinating finished works and works-in-progress, built-in storage cabinets and bookcases, lots of books, comfort-able furniture, and the old typewriter on which he still prefers to write. Dressed informally and without shoes, Gould graciously invited me into his office and answered all my specific questions, save those related to his immediate family. Not willing to react to a general question, Gould punctuated our interview with the cour-teous and gently spoken admonition, "Be more specific."

The holder of more than two dozen honorary degrees; a char-ter recipient (1981) of a MacArthur Foundation Prize Fellowship (a "genius award," as they have come to be known); the winner of numerous literary, scholarly, and scientific awards; and the author of 15 books, Gould was pleased to begin the interview with remarks about his own early education. But he cautioned, "I spent more time playing stickball in the street than I ever did reading when I was a kid."

Stephen Jay Gould is a product of New York City's public schools in their golden age from the late 1940s to about 1960 — the days when the system was filled with "older teachers who had gotten their jobs in the Thirties, in the Depression, many of them overqualified, some of them even Ph.D.s." His second book of essays, *The Panda's Thumb*, is dedicated to three of his best elementary school teachers, one of whom — Esther Ponti, his fifth-grade teacher — Gould corresponded with "until she died a few years ago." Looking back, Gould says he appreciated Ponti's dedication, toughness, imagination, and especially her willing-ness to accommodate youngsters with a developing passion for science. "She didn't know much science, and there was little sci-ence in the curriculum then. When she realized many of us were interested in science, she would set aside a time each week for us to sit in the back of the room and talk about science. She'd provide materials and books."

When Gould recalls his finest public school teachers, he talks frequently of their dedication to students and their unwavering adherence to high standards. Ted Weinkranz, a history teacher, was a "compassionate man, a committed intellectual." Jean Gollobin, a choral teacher, was "an extraordinarily committed human being who believed in excellence." Again and again, Gould refers to compassion and rigor as the twin characteristics of those teachers he recollects with greatest fondness. His descriptions of his parents are similar. He refers to his mother as a "brave woman and a wise owl" (dedication to *Hen's Teeth and Horse's Toes*) whose devotion to family touched her son; his father, a man of no great education, was nevertheless "an autodidact, a very learned man."

High excellence is the centerpiece of Gould's most enthusiastic memory of public school. "My greatest high school experience was singing in the all-city high school chorus. Peter Wilhousky would get together 250 kids from all over the city, the most motley mixture you ever saw — Italian kids from Staten Island, Puerto Rican kids from Manhattan, black kids from Harlem, all of whom liked to sing — and somehow welded us into an almost professional group. We sang once a year in Carnegie Hall."

After high school, Gould found himself at Antioch College, in Yellow Springs, Ohio. It was a new and welcome experience for a New York City boy. "It was a great pleasure to be in a place where the class size was never more than 30 and often fewer than 10," he reminisces. Antioch was also a place dedicated to writing. In high school, Gould recalls, classes were big, and teachers had five or six classes each day, making it impossible for them to read long essays, "but at Antioch we wrote for every single course, even physics courses. It was just understood that writing was essential." After graduation, Gould knew he had to go to Columbia University, so he could study paleontology at the American Museum of Natural History. In those days, the museum "had ties" to Columbia. From age five, he knew that he wanted to be a paleontologist. "Virtually any paleontologist who grew up in New York City will tell you the same story about going to the Museum of Natural History and loving the dinosaurs." Gould received his Ph.D. in 1967, four years out of Antioch, and landed a job at Harvard as an assistant professor.

Gould's spectacular career in science writing began rather modestly. "I got a call from Alan Ternes in 1973, the editor of *Natural History* magazine, and he asked me if I'd write a few columns." At the time, Gould didn't even know that the magazine had regular columns. For the first 10 years of his professional career, he had written basically "technical scientific papers, but I wrote them in an oddly literate style because it seemed the right way to me. Developing a career in more general writing was never an explicit intention." But it is something that just grew and grew. Now, 260 essays later, seven of Gould's books are collections of his best essays. *The Panda's Thumb* won a National Book Award in 1981; the original version of *The Mismeasure of Man* won the National Book Critics Circle Award in 1982; *Wonderful Life* was nominated and became a finalist for the Pulitzer Prize in 1991 and was honored by Phi Beta Kappa and Rhone-Poulenc in Britain as the best science book of the year. All of Gould's 15 books have sold well among serious readers. His writing is stylistically glorious, but his essays assume a reader's willingness to engage seriously with demanding ideas.

The book that comes closest to being an "education" book is, of course, *The Mismeasure of Man* (1981), in which Gould rejects "the idea that there's an effectively immutable, single factorial general intelligence." The book was reissued in 1996 in a revised and expanded edition, which serves as a highly informed refutation of *The Bell Curve* (1994) by Richard Herrnstein and Charles Murray, a work that favors the unitary interpretation of intelligence. Gould is absolutely certain that *The Bell Curve* is more about politics than science. "When the political pendulum shifts to the right, all these marginal viewpoints become momentarily respectable again. There's always a Murray and a Herrnstein. To get as much notice as it did, it had to strike a political chord, and its publication came just with the transition to the Gingrich Congress. . . . If you want to cut governmental spending, you're going to go with the argument that these people can't be helped because they're made that way," he says. Gould is particularly rankled by Murray's pretension to be a disinterested scholar when everyone knows he's a "conservative ideologue who's been in the employ of right-wing think tanks for 20 years." There is no real intellectual debate here, he argues, any more than there is for creationism. But these issues surface every time they become politically useful. Despite his long record of doing so, Gould does not believe that reacting against marginal theories is the best way for a scholar to spend his time, "but you can't just let [such theories] sit. It's frustrating."

Modern culture is also frustrating to Gould. While both graduate and undergraduate students at Harvard are extremely bright and motivated, they have no shared culture, which makes every form of teaching more difficult. "There really isn't any centerpiece of knowledge you can assume people to have. Even a generation ago, you could assume that the most common Shakespearean and Biblical quotations would be recognized by most students — but you just can't anymore." Gould is not convinced that there ever was a golden age for broad cultural knowledge, but he misses the relatively narrow, yet dependable culture that the generations shared until very recently.

Contemporary culture is filled with "sound bites, simplification, and short takes. In politics you can't discuss anything of substance," he charges. Gould is genuinely concerned about how people use what is available through online computer services. The paradox is that anything you want is just a few keystrokes away, but "what you get is a pretty picture, a paragraph, a song, and directions for how to dig deeper, which most people are disinclined to do." A large majority of Harvard students are ignorant of any historical perspective, cannot read in a foreign language, and, worst of all, will not look deeply into references "because they're not used to doing that," Gould says. He tells of a student who speculated about the origin of the word "real" but had no idea that "there was an etymological section in the dictionary" that would have yielded the information she wanted. Even the brightest and most motivated students in the land are a reflection of a culture that has no apparent center and no driving impulse toward thorough scholarship.

Gould has general opinions on what constitutes good public education, but he argues that his views are neither "deep nor distinctive." He favors small classes, a rigorous curriculum, and some common body of knowledge that includes basic grammar, arithmetic, Shakespeare, and the Bible as literature. He's opposed to teaching values in the school, other than such basic standards as golden-rule behavior, antiracism, and antisexism. Indeed, he hopes for a world in which "the fact that a child has black skin is no more consequential than having black or brown hair." In his own teaching, and particularly with graduate students, he tries to "nurture and foster an intellectual environment. . . . You have to project the importance of intellectual values and integrity, and do it by example."

It is when he talks about excellence that great passion infuses his voice. "I have strong feelings about intellectual integrity, doing things for yourself, not accepting what you're told, reading as much as you can in original sources, in original languages if you need to. Otherwise, you're just recycling what was given to you." His intellectual heroes are such towering scholars as Peter Medawar and Isaiah Berlin, to whom he dedicated *An Urchin in a Storm*. These men seemed to know everything, had great expertise in their chosen fields, and were absolutely dedicated to the highest ideals of scholarship. Both were polymaths and great models for young scholars. However, it is not academic work that draws Gould's highest praise, but excellence — high excellence in any responsible work, including scholarship. And Gould is well aware of the "rarity of the pursuit of excellence."

Watching people perform at the pinnacle of excellence in "anything" — be it opera, athletics, or scholarship — is what Gould most enjoys. Any reader of Stephen Jay Gould knows that baseball occupies a special place in his heart. Watching Ted Williams

at bat years ago or Wade Boggs today is a great thrill for
Professor Gould. But it is the Yankee Clipper who sets the gold
standard for what constitutes the pursuit of excellence. "My boy-
hood hero was Joe DiMaggio more than anyone else. I met him
once; he's a man of little talk but enormous action. His excellence
was on a baseball field, and he was gracious and elegant. He was
an artist at bat, and he didn't make compromises in the field,"
Gould says. Mutatis mutandis, he could be describing himself.

Photograph courtesy of the office of Dr. James P. Comer.

James P. Comer

I've written twice about James Comer, first in Educational Leadership *in September 1990 and again in the* Phi Delta Kappan *in March 1997. The first interview was conducted at the Yale Club in New York City; the second was in Comer's office at Yale's Child Study Center in New Haven, Connecticut. While Jim Comer was steadfast about his interest in child development and the crucial role it had to play in any school reform effort, there was one sharp difference between the two interviews.*

In the first interview, conducted during a recession, Comer hardly mentioned economic issues. In the second interview, the economic well-being of minority families was very much on Comer's mind because the economy of the nation was in a sustained and extremely strong phase. Comer had become convinced, as had several other African-American leaders from Jesse Jackson to Hugh Price, that the pivotal issue was now economic integration, and perhaps always had been that. School improvement was no less important; but until minority families participated fully in the American economy, there would be no real integration, no serious progress in any social or educational sphere.

James P. Comer, Maurice Falk Professor of Child Psychiatry at Yale University, associate dean of the Yale School of Medicine, director of the Yale University Child Study Center School Development Program, and one of the nation's chief architects for school change, is a child of poverty, but not of deprivation. His mother worked as a domestic in East Chicago, Indiana; but Maggie Comer understood that "education was a chance for a better life for her five children." Comer's father, a church-centered man, "was a very strong moral figure" in Comer's life; but he

Originally published as "Maintaining a Focus on Child Development: An Interview with Dr. James P. Comer" in *Phi Delta Kappan* (March 1997). Used with permission.

became ill when James was a boy, and his mother carried the burden of raising the family. Though the Comers were poor, there was no deprivation, because Maggie Comer watched what the educated, well-to-do women for whom she worked did and then imitated them, taking her children to the Museum of Science and Industry and to the Field Museum in Chicago. She also learned how to use telephone contacts and personal contacts in the schools to make good things happen for her children.

The period from the late 1930s to the mid-1950s, when Comer went through public school and started college, was a time that will never return. "I came out of a church community, a small town, a black community that was functioning well. It was before suburbanization and a lot of television. It was during a time of improved race relations, and I got a lot of support from teachers, all white." Several outstanding black students from his community went off to Indiana University and did well; they were role models for James and his siblings. But many others, "just as bright, just as able," did not do well at all. Comer wanted to understand what was going on, "what was it about the larger systems, and where could you make a difference for young people who were not receiving the support they needed?"

After he graduated from Indiana University in 1956, Comer attended Howard University College of Medicine, intending to be a general practitioner; but the plight of impoverished children and the realization that many of the patients he saw needed something other than traditional medicine nagged at him. Comer served his military obligation as a physician in the Public Health Service and then earned a master's degree in administration and mental health at the University of Michigan, partly as a way to give himself time to think. He soon realized, "I needed to know more about behavior, and that led me to psychiatry. I needed to know more about children, and that led me into child psychiatry." Having done most of his work in psychiatry at Yale, it seemed natural for Comer to make his career there. He knew with great certitude that he needed to work with children, that in the absence of a substantial and well-functioning community for many black youngsters he would need to work in schools, and that "part of what we had to do was create a community in the schools."

In 1968 Comer took responsibility for a Yale Child Study Center program in concert with the New Haven (Connecticut) public school system. The purpose of the program was to apply the principles of psychiatry and the behavioral sciences to the vexing problems of inner-city education.

The original program served two elementary schools, both in low-income, heavily black areas and both with abysmal records in the areas of academic achievement, attendance, and student behavior. Comer set out to establish "a governance and management team in each building that was representative of all the adult players — parents, teachers, administrators, custodians." Thus the program gave all the adults with a stake in a given school a chance to help build the school community. Over a period of years, the program grew to include the identification of learning obstacles; the delivery of programs focused on children, staff, and parents that fostered educational, social, and psychological development; and, increasingly, the infusion of elements that capitalized on the growing sense of the school as a community. "We demonstrated that just by changing the climate we could improve performance."

The Martin Luther King Jr. Elementary School is an example of the success of this approach. One of the two original schools, its students had been 19 months below grade level in language arts and 18 months below grade level in mathematics in 1968-69. By 1979 the scores in both areas (as measured by the Iowa Tests of Basic Skills) were at grade level, and by 1984 they were 12 months above grade level. No socioeconomic change had taken place in the community, but attendance was much improved, serious behavior problems were down dramatically, parent participation was high, and staff turnover was "almost nonexistent." Based on good results in several schools, the New Haven public schools decided to use the Comer School Development Project in all district schools.

A project originally designed to last five years took a decade to take firm root, as Comer and his staff learned how best to use their talents and how complex and nearly intractable some of the problems were. The community approach defeats the attitude expressed by a first-grader in the original project, who told his teacher on the first day of school, "Teacher, my momma said I don't have to do anything you say." Comer quickly learned that it was unusual to have a resident psychiatrist in the schools and that his role had to be that of provider of guidelines, information, inspiration, and administrative support.

As the School Development Project progressed, Comer and his staff learned that the original idea that has in many places evolved into school-based management was not comprehensive enough. They discovered nine operational elements that, Comer says, "remain the heart of my work today." Three "mechanisms" under-gird the program in any school: a governance and management team, a mental health or school support team, and a parents' program. The management team creates and supervises three critical education operations: a comprehensive school plan, an assessment program, and a staff development program. In addition, there is a three-part philosophy that pervades all the work: no fault (concentrate on solving problems), no decisions except by consensus, and no paralysis (no naysayer can stand in the way of a strong majority). The entire school community learns that the essential culture must be "a cooperative, learning, trying, experimenting attitude rather than an obstructive, adversarial relationship."

Today, the Comer training program, called the Comer Project for Change in Education, is operating in "more than 600 schools in 82 school districts in 26 states" — from New York and Maryland to North Carolina and California. Dissemination through training became important as the original staff members learned that they could not "be all over the place." Regional dissemination began in 1980, and national diffusion began in 1982. In addition to the original training center at Yale and one in Prince George's County, Maryland, there are now training centers at Cleveland State University, San Francisco State University, and Southern University of New Orleans. The Ford, Rockefeller, and Melville Foundations have provided support to help make the Comer Project for Change in Education a reality. Finally, the

Comer Project works with other reform and innovation efforts, such as Theodore Sizer's Coalition of Essential Schools, Howard Gardner's Project Zero, Janet Whitla's Educational Development Center, and Edward Zigler's Schools for the 21st Century in an endeavor to provide precisely those elements of change required in a particular school or school district.

The results of the Comer Project continue to be good, and regular assessments of several kinds are done to monitor progress. In New Orleans, for instance, which has a school/university partnership, several standardized measures are used along with a variety of ethnographic techniques. The New Orleans effort is still young, and Comer learned long ago that problems that at first seem intractable can yield to good will and hard work — but not rapidly. However, early evaluations of the first four project schools in New Orleans show a "general positive trend." In four years many students have moved from the 30th to the 50th percentile in reading and mathematics, and the ethnographic work indicates that "a rigorous system of monitoring student performance and growth . . . may have accounted for the significant improvement observed in student performance." When the school becomes a community, when goals and programs are established, and when there is both a determination to make progress and a will to assess that progress, motivation to improve is high.

James Comer is a thoughtful man, a man who weighs what he says and who has lived long enough to recall serious national economic problems, wars, and cataclysmic social change. His views on what deeply ails the culture and the schools have taken shape over a long career that took him from poverty in East Chicago to a moment on Martha's Vineyard where President Clinton stood for a picture with one arm on Comer's shoulder and the other on Comer's late wife's shoulder. Soon Comer will publish a new book, *Waiting for a Miracle: Schools Are Not the Problem.* It is clear to him that such issues as school reform and school integration are not the pivotal problems. "The black community allowed the media to define the issue. School segregation was only a symbol. It was a symbol of inferiority that had to be destroyed, but the media allowed people to focus on that as the issue rather than on economic integration."

There was a time, 35 years ago and earlier, when a relatively uneducated worker could "enter the job market and get a job that would take care of a family." At some point around 1960, that began to be less true. The notion that the economy required some winners and many losers became dominant, and "the most marginal, vulnerable families" suffered the most. Many of those families were black. Industry and many middle-class people left the cities, and no tax resources moved in to replace those losses for the people who remained behind. Black youngsters were undereducated, and employers used the lack of education as a proxy for work readiness and did not hire these young people. "Many of the problems we have — teenage pregnancy, violence, crime, and the like — are really outgrowths of families' not being able to do their job because [the parents] aren't educated well enough or they are excluded from good jobs."

Too many black children from families under economic and social stress are not prepared to go to school, and the schools are not fully ready for them when they do arrive. In some urban districts, up to half of the teachers are not qualified to do their jobs, and 24% of all the students in this country attend 1% of the schools — basically, in the 100 largest cities. "The families are under stress, the districts are under stress, and their ability to prepare these kids for mainstream life is limited," Comer says. He would like to see more communities adopt rigorous standards, but he insists that "opportunity standards" also be provided. You can't provide inner-city students with overcrowded classes, deteriorating buildings, many unqualified teachers, and far too few modern books, supplies, computers, and lab equipment and then say that they must meet very high standards.

The black community must take considerable responsibility and form "a coalition or a federation that focuses on the essential issues of education and economic opportunity — inclusion in the economic system." Such figures as Hugh Price of the Urban League, Marion Wright Edelman of the Children's Defense Fund, and Kweisi Mfume of the NAACP (National Association for the Advancement of Colored People) must seize this initiative, in Comer's view. Louis Farrakhan is not an important player in this effort, Comer argues. "He tapped into the unrest, the anger, and the desire to do something, but it could have been done by anybody with enough visibility."

Comer is convinced that "it is economic integration that allows groups to come together in meaningful ways that then make school integration possible." There has to be more interest in the well-being of the group and not just the individual, more investment in and concern for human capital. And the reason is easily understood: "if you have enough individuals who are not functioning well, you have a society that is going to decline." The lack of support for urban schools may be legal, but it is also immoral. The hardest-hit schools must be provided with adequate funds and the leadership to do the job well, and a structure must be created that is "beyond politics." All the leaders in our society must understand that "if many families cannot function, we cannot have a world-class education system."

For nearly 30 years James Comer has been a consistent voice for child development and the well-being of all children, but especially poor children. His achievements and honors are extraordinary: physician, Yale professor, columnist for *Parents Magazine,* special awards and singular honors by the dozen, 36 honorary degrees, five books, more than 100 scholarly articles, trustee of the Carnegie Foundation, and more. But he is proudest of the laser-like, unwavering focus that he has kept on putting what we know about how children grow and develop at the center of all work related to the very young.

"I have maintained a steady focus on child development and the importance of considering that. This is what I have tried to bring to education," he says. "Even people in education who are sensitive to child development focus on curriculum/instruction/assessment first, and I argue that it should be development first and that development should guide everything else."

Photograph by Timothy Greenfield-Sanders.

E.D. Hirsch Jr.

When it comes to public relations, E.D. (Don) Hirsch Jr. is his own worst enemy. By his own admission, Don Hirsch is a polemicist by nature. He so enjoys the role of agitator and maverick that he often does not represent his views and accomplishments as accurately or positively as he might.

Don Hirsch is a very reasonable man, not nearly as doctrinaire as he sometimes presents himself in writing. During a long interview and later over lunch at a Chinese restaurant in Charlottesville, Virginia, where Hirsch lives, he revealed many facts about Core Knowledge and Cultural Literacy that surprised me.

Don Hirsch insisted only that half of the elementary curriculum follow the Core Knowledge outline; easily agreed that teachers can and should use any methods, including progressive techniques, that work (that is, yield measurable results); and spoke about the efforts he had made in recent years to include many minority authors, historical events, and issues in the Core Knowledge curriculum. He questioned me about my relatively gentle writing and said, "You're just not a polemicist. I am."

Many educators first heard of E.D. Hirsch in 1987, when *Cultural Literacy* was published. But Don Hirsch's interest in K-12 education predates that book's publication by more than a decade. In the late 1970s, E.D. Hirsch Jr. had a professional experience that "shook me up and changed my life." Already a full professor of English, holder of an endowed chair at the University of Virginia, and the author of five scholarly books and many articles, Hirsch had become interested in how students read and write and what the foundations are for those skills. As part of a study he conducted, he gave reading samples to students at a

Originally published as "Doing What Works: An Interview with E.D. Hirsch, Jr." in *Phi Delta Kappan* (September 1997). Used with permission.

community college in Richmond and to students at the University of Virginia. He soon discovered that "the kids at the community college in Richmond could read — could decode — just as well as the kids at the University of Virginia. They just couldn't understand as many texts."

Hirsch discerned that it wasn't the decoding skills that presented problems for the mostly black youngsters at the community college. "It was the prior knowledge they brought to the page," he says.

The particular incident that shook Hirsch to his intellectual foundations was the assignment of a passage on Lee's surrender to Grant at Appomattox Court House. "The university students read it with ease," he recalls. "The community college people could not read it, because they had no idea who Lee was, who Grant was, what the context was — and in Richmond, Virginia!" This result, so surprising to Hirsch, fit perfectly with developments in psycholinguistics in the 1960s and 1970s that showed that background is critical to reading, that literacy is not an abstract skill, and that "the tool metaphor of education," as Hirsch calls it, "is actually incorrect."

In 1944, when Don Hirsch was a 16-year-old growing up in Memphis, "in the highly segregated South," Gunnar Myrdal's enormously influential book, *An American Dilemma,* was published. Reading the book made clear to young Don for the first time that racism was a serious deterrent to democracy. He recalls Myrdal's book as "the single book that made the greatest impression on me." Although both the general Southern culture and his own prosperous family had taught him that the status quo must be preserved, "I disobeyed all those rules after I read this book." Hirsch argues that much of his concern with progressive education and its ill effects grows out of his social conscience and his deep belief that "avoidable injustice" must be eradicated. It is simply not fair for schools to withhold from disadvantaged children the background knowledge that the most successful advantaged students accumulate from their homes and, to varying degrees, from their schools over a period of years.

Teachers College at Columbia University and its two great education leaders of the 1920s and the 1930s, John Dewey and William Heard Kirkpatrick, are in Hirsch's view unwitting villains. In fact, both Dewey and Kirkpatrick believed in high standards, and Hirsch is quick to acknowledge that, "when they work, progressive methods are superb. It's a big mistake to read my books as being anti-progressive methods. What they're 'anti' about is what Dewey himself said about such methods: these methods are great as long as the kids learn." Hirsch is distressed that the progressive "project method" is often not carefully monitored to see whether students are actually learning. He is particularly troubled by the "anti-subject-matter orientation" of progressive education, in which many upper-middle-class youngsters succeed because they get so much education and information at home, whereas students from "uneducated backgrounds are going to get needed information only from school," and they're not getting it.

Hirsch contends that children really attend two schools: "the home-school and the school-school." Middle-class students get a good education in the home-school, "which makes up for some of the deficiencies in the content-poor school-school. Disadvantaged kids have a poor home-school — content-poor as far as academic knowledge goes — and they also attend a content-poor school-school." This "social justice gap" is of greater concern to Hirsch than the fact that the middle-class students could be doing better if their schools were good, though he believes that they deserve better schools, too. From Hirsch's point of view, most elementary schools have a fragmented and incoherent curriculum. There is too much emphasis on such "tool skills" as accessing information, critical thinking, cooperative learning, and problem-solving skills and far too little emphasis on solid academic content taught in tandem with those skills that are needed to learn the content. He further argues that "the research literature offers not one example of successful implementation of progressivist methods in a carefully controlled longitudinal study," and therefore, he argues, it is time to cast off the progressive, anti-subject-matter ideas that have kept educators in thrall for seven decades.

In the early 1980s, Hirsch began to investigate what educated people in our society actually know. Several beliefs provided the underpinning for this project. First, "background knowledge is critical to understanding, and this knowledge has to be shared in order for communication to take place." Second, background knowledge is continually changing and always needs to be updated, though not dramatically. "It's like a battleship. It doesn't turn in the water instantly. There's always considerable overlap between generations in a literate culture." Third, a democracy cannot function well unless the schools take care of providing background knowledge. This is simply a core fact of social justice. Finally, "if you're not broadly knowledgeable, you are less able to learn new, unexpected things." Hirsch believes that the progressive motto, "learning to learn," is accurate. "Unfortunately, it is interpreted as just learning critical-thinking skills and empty abstract skills." Hirsch is not critical of any of the progressive methods, so long as they are based on content. "If you know something about a subject, you can build on that fast to learn something else. I doubt there's a cognitive psychologist who would disagree with that."

One of Hirsch's most severe criticisms is directed toward the curriculum of American elementary schools. "I assumed that there was a curriculum in the schools. What you find out is that this is a myth. Kids in the same school building in the second grade are learning very different things from kids in another second grade in the same building." One teacher does a long unit on dinosaurs, while another teacher spends a month on farm animals, and a third spends the same time teaching about machinery. This means that the students get no common preparation for the next grade, and the situation is simply a disaster for children who move to a new school or district. "The kids who are most disadvantaged are those who are moving around, and they move mostly within a single district. They need to have at least a solid core curriculum." Unlike students in, say, Switzerland, youngsters move quite frequently in the United States — from school to school, from town to town, and from state to state.

The Core Knowledge Foundation in Charlottesville, Virginia, the organization that publishes materials for an elementary core curriculum, is housed in a small Tudor building shared with two realtors, an insurance agency, and some licensed massage therapists. It is a rabbit warren of small rooms, housing eight employees and thousands of books and pieces of curricular material illustrating what is commercially available to children. The goal of the foundation is to supply the core knowledge in a fairly simple form for half of the curriculum. "If we said the core was 100%, we know that that would not be politically acceptable. Furthermore, it's not necessary. This is a very solid 50%. If kids know this material — and we now have evidence about its cumulative effect — then it's fine for localities to add whatever interests they have or for the teacher to add whatever interests he or she has."

Schools from San Antonio to the South Bronx are reporting improved test scores, higher attendance rates, greater student enthusiasm, and increased collaboration among teachers who share and appreciate clear content guidelines. James Coady, principal of the Morse School in Cambridge, Massachusetts, states that, "with the acquisition of the Core Knowledge curriculum, our scores have jumped, really jumped. We were always in the middle of the schools in our division, but now we are in the top quartile and often the number-one or number-two school in a category."

In 1987, when *Cultural Literacy* was published, some readers criticized it as elitist and too strongly oriented toward whites and Europeans. Hirsch sees that charge as a red herring. He never argued that the curriculum must be static, only that there should be a common body of knowledge in order to have consistency, to create a level playing field for all students, and to ensure that moving from school to school did not invite educational trauma. In fact, in 1988 Hirsch assembled a multicultural committee in Charlottesville to advise him, including Henry Louis Gates Jr., Elizabeth Fox-Genovese, experts on Native American history, and specialists on Latino culture. "I mean, we didn't have the Lithuanians, but we did have 24 working groups," he recalls. "You had to persuade your subgroup that something was worth including. The core had to be realistic. If you're going to add something, you need to give up something. You can't make fourth-graders learn everything." The core-curriculum draft that came out of that 1988 meeting was then made the subject of a much larger conference in 1990, and out of that came the core curriculum that remains pretty much intact today.

Hirsch has also often been criticized for the methods he suggests. It is true that he favors whole-class instruction most of the time and sees nothing wrong with drill and practice. "It works in football and in piano playing, so why should it work everywhere except in math and English?" he wonders. But E.D. Hirsch is primarily interested in results. "I don't believe there's any one right way in teaching. It's such a complex act, the interchange between children and a teacher, that it would be a grave mistake to impose a monolithic method on the teacher." What he demands is accountability and demonstrable results based on a content-filled core curriculum. "I'm a pragmatist, and I'll welcome any method that truly works."

To learn what should be included in that draft curriculum, Hirsch and his colleagues "did a lot of testing. We were actually quite scientific in trying to get the range of this knowledge that successful people knew in common." The four years of testing with parents, educators, students, education organizations, other stakeholders, and experts, along with the 1990 convocation, form the foundation of the *Core Knowledge Sequence* and a series of resource books with such titles as *What Your First-Grader Needs to Know* and *What Your Fifth-Grader Needs to Know.* This material is clear, detailed, and very concrete.

Hirsch rejects curricular guidelines that say such things as children in first grade should identify beliefs and value systems of specific groups. He much prefers the specificity of such guidelines as: introduce ancient civilizations and the variety of religions in the world, using maps of the ancient world. Topics are Egypt: King Tutankhamen, Nile River, pyramids, mummies, animal gods, hieroglyphics; Babylonia: Tigris and Euphrates, Hammurabi; Judaism: Moses, Passover, Chanukah; Christianity: Jesus; Arabia:

Mohammed, Allah, Islam; India: Indus River, Brahma, Hinduism, Buddha; China: Yellow River, Confucius, Chinese New Year.

The teacher is assumed to be generally knowledgeable but also willing to learn along the way. Helpful materials are provided, and the extreme vagueness of a "politically unobjectionable" but essentially empty guideline is avoided.

Almost every state is now working on standards for higher achievement, and there is currently great interest in E.D. Hirsch's work. The sixth National Core Knowledge Conference was held in Denver in March 1997. Some 1,300 people attended, a great increase from the 50 who attended the first conference held six years earlier. More than 400 schools in 40 states now use the core curriculum, and that number grows by several schools each month. Yet Don Hirsch remains bemused by the education establishment's early and virulent rejection of *Cultural Literacy.* There was a "strong discrediting campaign saying the book was 'trivial pursuit' and Eurocentric." Both the *Harvard Educational Review* and *Teachers College Record* ran strongly negative reviews — the *Record* running "two slashing reviews in one issue."

Hirsch's newest book, *The Schools We Need and Why We Don't Have Them* (Doubleday, 1996), has largely been ignored by the education community, though it received good reviews in the *New York Times,* the *American School Board Journal,* and the popular press. Early in 1997, Hirsch had what the *Los Angeles Times* called "a triumphal visit to Harvard," which causes him to believe that the consistent message espoused by his movement is very much in tune with the country today. Yet when I contacted Hirsch to do this interview, so convinced is he that the general education community still wishes to shun him that he expressed doubt that the piece would actually be published.

Don Hirsch is a welcoming, friendly man who is more than a little frustrated by all the criticism he has received from professional educators. He believes that it is the essence of common sense to reject the idea that critical thinking consists in mastering a set of abstract procedures, as opposed to, say, learning how to think critically by analyzing the contradiction between the principle of equality expressed in the Declaration of Independence and the existence of slavery when the Declaration was written. He respects and welcomes Robert Slavin's "careful research and scholarship" on reading, but he rejects Alfie Kohn's "highly romantic and scientifically unaccepted" notions about how children should be rewarded and disciplined. Quite simply, Hirsch wants every elementary school to have a core curriculum "that is based on what really works, that is demanding and rich, that is coherent, and that all elementary students can be exposed to." If that were the reality through grade 8, Hirsch would favor a more flexible system in the upper grades, in which students could follow their own intellectual bents.

While Hirsch continues to see himself as a maverick and certainly outside the mainstream in education, he remains utterly convinced of his beliefs and is beginning to warm to the idea that expert sentiment is moving his way. "In the basic elements of the reasoning behind *Cultural Literacy* and the new book, I really don't believe I'm wrong. You're interviewing me, and the *Kappan* is willing to publish the article, because there has been a movement in my direction." People want a coherent, clear curriculum based on solid content.

Hirsch told me that his primary influence was his father, who taught him to "follow a conviction even if it's not what the crowd believes." So young Don entered the navy, stood for political liberalism, rejected his father's prosperous cotton brokerage business, became an academic, married a professor's daughter, and raised three children with her. And throughout his long academic career he has followed his deepest intellectual beliefs and convictions. Hirsch contends that his work was never refuted on scientific grounds; the objections were always oddly ideological or moral. "Teachers, who have always wanted what is best for children," he says, "are now ready to hear my view: Let's do what works."

Claudio Sanchez

I interviewed Claudio Sanchez on a warm day in Washington, D.C., in the outdoor rooftop dining area of the National Public Radio (NPR) building. Because of the noise from the surrounding streets several stories below us, I had to lean in to hear Sanchez, adding a certain intimacy to the interview.

While Sanchez was willing to answer any questions I asked about his biography or work as an education reporter, he continually and fairly quickly returned to the themes of his own upbringing in Mexico and Arizona and the plight of so many Latino youngsters in the United States. I have heard Claudio Sanchez on NPR several times since our meeting and am always struck by the poignancy of many of his stories of poverty and unfairness and disparity between rich and poor.

Sanchez covers all sorts of education stories in his work for NPR, but much like the interview, he continually returns to the theme of injustice in the schools for poor Americans, and often Latino Americans. Claudio Sanchez is a drum major for closing the gap between advantaged and disadvantaged students. He does not have a bully pulpit, but NPR is a pretty good one.

Claudio Sanchez is the education correspondent for National Public Radio (NPR), the nonprofit network of 540 member stations that 17.1 million Americans listen to each week. Since February 1989 Sanchez has covered education stories for NPR that touch on federal and local policies, breaking news and features, and reform issues in elementary, secondary, and higher education. While Sanchez covers a range of stories about young people and education, much of his work focuses on the plight of poor families, underprivileged students, and Latino culture.

Originally published as "Bringing the Voices of the People to the People: An Interview with Claudio Sanchez" in *Phi Delta Kappan* (April 1998). Used with permission.

Sanchez is the product of a Mexican-American family of very limited means who made the transition to American culture with considerable success.

Born in Nogales, Sonora, Mexico, in 1954, Sanchez grew up in a rich cultural mix of Mexican and American influences. Nogales, Sonora, is directly across the border from Nogales, Arizona, and in the Fifties and Sixties it was "easy to cross back and forth. I grew up with 'Dennis the Menace' and 'Leave it to Beaver' on our television set." While Claudio was still in early elementary school, his parents divorced, and his mother and older brother became the primary influences on him. Claudio's father had legally moved the family to the United States before the divorce, but his mother and her four children, three boys and a girl, had never actually moved. After completing elementary school in Mexico, Sanchez did move to Nogales, Arizona, with his mother and siblings, and there he attended and graduated from the local high school.

Young Claudio benefited from the dual influences of trips back to Mexico and life in the United States. His aunts and other relatives — but especially his older brother, who was then attending the National University of Mexico — acquainted him with Latino life and the possibilities for a future in Mexico. At the same time Claudio experienced American values and saw the possibilities of life in the United States.

School was a central part of Claudio's life. "Education was never in doubt. I did well; I read a lot because of my mother, and I didn't find the transition to an American school difficult" — in large part, he recalls, because he was completely bilingual. His father had moved to California and was not a strong influence, which was one of the main reasons for his mother's move to the United States, a country where a single woman could raise a family without being "talked about by women in dark shawls as they walked to and from Mass." It was his mother's hard work and profound belief in education that sustained the three children at home, as well as the example of his brother, who, by the time Claudio began high school, had graduated from the National

University of Mexico and was doing well in business in his homeland.

When it came time to choose a college, Claudio was pulled toward Mexico by his brother and toward the United States by his school counselors. Eventually he opted to go to Northern Arizona University in Flagstaff. "I liked Northern Arizona University because it was so small. The National University of Mexico had over 100,000 students. I thought, the smaller the college, the better my chances for doing well." With the sponsorship of an influential teacher at Northern Arizona, Guy Bensusan, Sanchez and some other students put together a radio program to create a local Spanish voice. It was Claudio's first experience with the medium. This was more a cultural adventure than a career pursuit for Sanchez, who was a print journalism major. "I left school convinced that my future was print. I thought radio was fun, but I really didn't understand that you could do terrific journalism in radio. Serious journalism had to be print."

After college, Sanchez considered entering business with his brother, and he tried a number of things ranging from teaching to radio reporting. He taught for two years at the Treehaven Boarding School in Tucson, Arizona, where "half of the students were wealthy and the other half very poor, but all of them had the same problem, which was neglect. They just didn't see their parents. Some were children of jet-setters, and others had been abused and were wards of the state." Sanchez was a live-in teacher who taught writing, English, and Spanish but also made breakfast, got the youngsters to brush their teeth, and coached them in soccer — that is, when he wasn't sponsoring the 4-H Club or taking students on hikes or driving the school van.

During the 1980s, Sanchez held a series of jobs in radio, starting in 1980 at KUAT, the public radio station at the University of Arizona, where, he says, "I still had reservations about radio reporting. By 1984, I discovered what I know now — that you can do serious, good journalism on the radio and that radio is the best of all worlds. You didn't have to paraphrase anyone but could let them speak for themselves. You could create scenes with sound, and production became very appealing to me, producing stories." Sanchez also did some high-quality radio documentary work with a "terrific independent producer, Sandy Tolan," and in 1988 he finally ended up at the Latin American News Service in El Paso, Texas, "the job that became the springboard" to his current post at NPR.

When the offer came from NPR, he hesitated. "I didn't want the job initially because they said I'd be reporting on education. I was upset that NPR didn't want to send a reporter to cover the Southwest, the area where I grew up and where there were terrific stories," he recalls. But he was assured that he would have the freedom to go beyond schools and that he could travel. The offer was irresistible, so Sanchez moved to Washington, D.C., NPR's headquarters, and soon asked the woman who became his wife to join him. Claudio Sanchez quickly learned that the emphasis at NPR was on quality and that he did have considerable latitude in selecting the stories he felt were important.

Periodically, Sanchez's education stories are about the Latino community. "I'm doing a story now about how immigrants are raising their kids these days. Why are Latinos dropping out of school? Why are Latinos undereducated?" He did a story in Virginia about an 11-year-old Latino boy who was an alcoholic and lived in an "awful neighborhood." Sanchez saw promise and hope in this boy, who desperately needed help with his school, family, and social problems. But no one could find a program for him. "There's no mystery why these kids are failing," Sanchez says. The issue is that we permit this boy to drift, and no one does more than apply an occasional bandage or supply some tired bromide to the problem. Schools must focus on their academic mission, and other caring agencies must make certain that students come to school ready to learn. "No amount of money or curriculum reform or toughening of academic standards will help so long as students are plagued by poverty, drugs, violence, crime, broken homes, and other social problems."

Sanchez has covered stories about issues related to young people that range from a Norplant program in Baltimore that is designed to prevent teen pregnancy to youngsters from "stable communities" who are just as depressed as poor kids, hang out at the same 7-Eleven stores, get some material comfort, but can't "find an adult who will take a real interest." He once did a story about a child who had a terrible record of violence, even fighting with some of his teachers as early as fifth grade. "He roamed free with no one applying any discipline," Sanchez says. Like a leitmotif, the issues of abandonment and inadequate care run through many of Claudio Sanchez's stories of young people.

I asked Sanchez whether he had looked at middle-class areas and schools recently. He spoke of a school in Indianapolis. "It was a clean school, wonderful classrooms and grounds — but little learning was going on." The students were middle-class white and black youngsters, but there was no academic culture in the school. No one said learning was important, so many students roamed around, and a typical teacher remark was "Let the day end, so I can leave here." From the principal to the teachers to the students, Sanchez found no inspiration, no strong sense of mission, and certainly no commitment to the academic life of the school.

Too often, Sanchez finds that "U.S. schools today don't know what their real function is. Their confusion reflects the confusion of the general society," he believes. From Mexico to France to Japan, the academic mission is clear, and "the surrogate parenting role and the health role" are the clear responsibilities of other agencies.

Of course, many stories could be told of students in elite or special schools who are doing well, and Sanchez does cover some of these. People constantly tell him that he shouldn't focus on unfortunate youngsters but should do more stories about students who win prizes and competitions. "Well, I love doing those stories because they pick me up, but I can't easily put aside the other stories." Sanchez is drawn to the small, revealing story of a student in some difficulty. "The best stories are the simple stories that tell about people," he says. "You create an opening for people to speak out, and you don't intrude. You just allow people to tell their story."

One of the most powerful stories Sanchez told me was about a girl and her reaction to President Bush's launching of an anti-drug campaign seven years ago. The President's speech was broadcast live into 15,000 secondary schools all across the country at noon. Sanchez arranged to be in the library of Joel Spingarn High School in Washington, D.C., during the broadcast.

The students listened attentively when the President said, "We have to get a handle on this, and you, the kids, are on the front line. Say no to drugs; help your friends and parents and others say no."

Sanchez then sat down with a group of boys and girls and asked them how they felt about what they had just heard. One girl, Felicia, simply broke down, saying her mother sends her and her little sister to sell drugs on a local corner. Her grandmother doesn't want to hear from her when she complains. Through tears and gulps, Felicia told Sanchez, "It sounds good to hear the President, but there's nothing I can do."

Bilingual education is an area in which Sanchez has done several stories and about which he has strong feelings. For instance, he did a piece on Coral Way Elementary School in Miami's "Little Havana." Bilingual education is an enrichment program there, not a remedial program. It works, and it is appealing to both Spanish-speaking and non-Spanish-speaking students. "I believe that bilingual education is as much a skill as reading and writing, one that this nation cannot overlook or underestimate. Bilingual education in too many places is remediation, and that's a bad model. I don't want classes to be conducted entirely in Spanish. Nothing should intrude on the development of the best English skills. Knowing English is a primary obligation."

Racism is a pervasive issue in America, and Sanchez has done a number of stories on this vexing problem. But unconscious bigotry worries Sanchez more than blatant racism does. He recently did a story about a team of teachers in Virginia who had been given special preparation to deal with difficult students. He sat in on a planning session and heard a team member proclaim that "the problem with these Latino parents is that they don't value education; they'd rather have their kids have babies — another person to work and bring in income." That is the sort of revealing statement that Sanchez believes will speak to his radio audience without any mediation on his part. He knew that his audience would understand that the attitude of that teacher "precludes her from seeing a Latino kid as capable. That person has already decided the parents are ill-equipped to raise that child." Sanchez is beginning to believe that class, even more than racism, may be the underlying issue in schools. "If school people in positions of authority and influence just don't think well of an entire class of people, such as struggling Latinos, then no one will expect them to learn," he says.

Some of the success stories that Sanchez has covered hearten him, but others make him angry. He spent time in a wonderful school in Columbus, Ohio, that had been underwritten by Apple Computer, Inc. "There's a high school that has wall-to-wall technology. Teachers have laptops, the library is high-tech, there's a computer for every two kids — wonderful projects going on," he recalled. Teachers and students were enthusiastic, and this school really was a model for what a successful school could be. The problem was that this "program existed only because Apple was funding it, and, because of its success, it was even attracting other outside money." When Sanchez went a short distance to visit another Columbus school, he found almost no technology. In its place were dispirited teachers who had been given training, but virtually no equipment. "It's a very perverse thing to create models that people aren't willing to duplicate. It creates expectations that can't be met."

While there is a strong focus on young people and schools in great difficulty in Sanchez's work, there are, fortunately, many bright spots. "A lot of harsh critics give me the benefit of the doubt because education is such a profoundly 'people story,' the story of children." Chester Finn, for instance, has a very different point of view from Sanchez's, but he rarely challenges him on a story when a child's emotions are included. After the Felicia story, CNN reporter Judy Woodruff phoned Sanchez to ask how she could be of personal help to that young girl. And Sanchez does occasionally do a story about a school program that really does make him hopeful.

"Seattle is improving the way youngsters learn math in middle school by looking at the way it's taught in elementary schools. Teachers are teaching other teachers to use a nurturing approach, but not a babying approach, in the George Washington Middle School that serves almost exclusively black and Latino students." What is impressive is that this program has the potential for duplication without great expense. Sanchez observed students voluntarily giving up recess to do more math. The students were doing a survey dealing with percentages and graphs, and the teachers were willing to work harder and longer and to include parents in their work. "The teachers in that building made the decision to do the extra work." The focus was on math, but it influenced the way everything else worked in that school.

Claudio Sanchez grew up in two cultures, saw his parents' marriage dissolve early in life, and watched his mother toil, often at two jobs, to keep her family together and to get her children educated. While he believes in hard work and individual enterprise, he understands from personal experience that there are times when decent but poor people need the help of the government as a last resort. "I saw my mother go on welfare for a year. It was a most hurtful thing for her. She was ashamed of it. Most people don't like to rely on government, but the fact that the help existed got us through. Poor people don't get enough credit for finding their way out of that."

Claudio Sanchez spends his working hours searching for stories that illustrate just that kind of travail, and he sometimes finds the voice of a child or teacher that shows the way out. He simply wants to provide the voices that will "allow listeners to decide whether something is right or wrong" and to help Americans feel outrage at the present system "of inequities between rich and poor schools which result in overcrowding, old textbooks and materials, and generally dilapidated conditions" for those youngsters who need the most attention, the best facilities, and the best teaching.

Mark Gearan

Everyone I interviewed was enthusiastic about her or his work, but Mark Gearan was certainly the proudest about the job he was doing. Again and again, Gearan extolled the virtues of the Peace Corps and told me how proud and fulfilled he felt to have this job — Director of the Peace Corps of the United States. As a long-time believer in the efficacy of government, as an Irish-Catholic son of Massachusetts (home of the Kennedy family), and as a devoted and loyal Kennedy-style Democrat, Mark Gearan felt that for him this was the perfect job in the perfect government agency.

The average length of service for a Peace Corps director is just under 2½ years. Mark Gearan served nearly four years before accepting the presidency at Hobart and William Smith Colleges, a small liberal arts college in Geneva, New York.

In September 1995, with his wife holding the Bible, Vice President Al Gore officiating, and a smiling President Clinton in the background, Mark Gearan was sworn in as the 14th director of the Peace Corps, which he calls "the best job in Washington." Gearan had worked in the rough-and-tumble presidential campaign of 1992 as Vice President Gore's campaign manager, had acted as deputy director of President Clinton's transition team, and had served for more than two years in the West Wing of the White House as an assistant to the President, director of communications, and White House deputy chief of staff. Nevertheless, he retains a bright and youthful enthusiasm for both government service in general and his work with the Peace Corps. Gearan speaks appreciatively of the Peace Corps as "an enormous national treasure" and of his own great good fortune "as an Irish

Originally published as "How Government Can Help People: An Interview with Mark Gearan" in *Phi Delta Kappan* (November 1998). Used with permission.

Catholic son of Massachusetts to have the chance to be part of the Peace Corps, President Kennedy's greatest legacy — a tremendous honor and privilege."

Mark Gearan was born in 1955 in Gardner, Massachusetts, into a family that valued education and public service. His mother served on the school committee, his father was a high school principal, and several close family members were classroom teachers or guidance counselors. Always interested in government, by age 12 Mark was leafleting for Fr. Robert Drinan, who served for 10 years as a member of the U.S. House of Representatives from Gearan's district. When he obtained his driver's license at 16, Gearan began driving for Father Drinan; and during his undergraduate years at Harvard he served as a summer intern in Drinan's Washington, D.C., office. By 1978, just out of college, he was working in Drinan's campaign as press secretary. "This thoughtful, committed political leader" was Gearan's first mentor in government service. Gearan recalls that Drinan showed him firsthand "what government could do and the difference it could make in people's lives. When you grow up in a small town, you get to see how government can help people."

From 1978 to 1995, Gearan had a succession of work experiences that prepared him extremely well for his current job. He served as press secretary and later chief of staff for Berkley Bedell, a representative from Iowa and "a wonderful member of Congress with great integrity." Gearan's knowledge of Iowa was a big help in his next job, working on the presidential campaign of Massachusetts Gov. Michael Dukakis. After that, he worked with the Democratic Governors' Association and came to know Gov. Richard Celeste of Ohio, who had served as director of the Peace Corps under President Carter. It was at this time that he also got to know the young governor of Arkansas. And this connection led to Gearan's campaign work in 1992 and to his subsequent White House assignments. "Virtually all of my working life has been in government service," Gearan says, noting the exception of a very short stint as a journalist. And each government job gave him contact with excellent mentors.

When Gearan learned in the early summer of 1995 that Carol Bellamy, the director of the Peace Corps, was moving to UNICEF, he asked for the job because it's "so singular in government." The Peace Corps was established by President Kennedy in March 1961 and has sent more than 160,000 volunteers to 132 countries over the past 37 years. The basic mission of the Peace Corps has never changed:

- to provide volunteers who contribute to the social and economic development of interested countries;
- to promote a better understanding of Americans among the people whom the volunteers serve; and
- to strengthen Americans' understanding of the world and its peoples.

"Education has always been at the heart of the work of Peace Corps volunteers," Gearan says. A fair amount of that educational effort goes into classroom teaching. Some 38% of the volunteers teach in foreign countries, the largest project of several that the Peace Corps undertakes. But the efforts in environment, health, business, and agriculture — the other major areas of emphasis — are also essentially educational. Volunteers receive 12 weeks of training, always in the host country. In groups of 20 to 50, the volunteers learn about the "language, technology, culture, and safety and security issues" of their host country. In addition, there is training in the specific area of their work. Classroom teachers, for instance, learn about the pedagogical techniques that have the best chance for success in Ghana or Paraguay or Uzbekistan. "The Peace Corps is not top-down but values the local culture and mores."

Volunteers know they will be carefully screened before they are accepted, a process that includes interviews and four letters of recommendation as well as medical and legal clearance. They're told this will be "the toughest job you'll ever love," a phrase that is virtually the slogan of the Peace Corps. Peace Corps service requires a commitment to three months of training and two years of work in a foreign country. The characteristics that make Peace Corps volunteers effective are essentially the same characteristics that educators frequently mention when they speak of prized or effective teachers. The volunteers' knowledge and use of English is excellent, and they often can write quite well. They have great energy for and commitment to their work. Indeed, a frequent comment from local residents is that "Peace Corps volunteers reinvigorated our professional lives." Finally, the volunteers are inquisitive about the local culture, problems, and issues. They "willingly ask questions, and they value discussion and team problem solving over lecture and memorization."

The influence the Peace Corps has had is inestimable. "So many of the leaders in business, commerce, and education in host countries were educated by Peace Corps volunteers," Gearan points out — "leaders such as the minister of agriculture in Eritrea or the ambassador from Ghana. The president of Chad came to Washington and thanked the Peace Corps for the difference it made to his country's education and health and then added that he was taught by a Peace Corps volunteer." The eradication of Guinea worm disease in several African countries, the work in education and health related to HIV and AIDS, and the construction of roads and bridges in many nations are representative examples of the accomplishments of the Peace Corps. Peace Corps volunteers "helped to write the first sign-language dictionary in Mongolian and English and environmental awareness textbooks for seventh-graders in Fiji." The bonds of friendship that are formed with local people often last for years, sometimes resulting in lifelong relationships.

While the "basic architecture of the Peace Corps endures," the organization is far from static. Like any other good education organization, the Peace Corps is working to prepare for the "challenges of the next century." The proper mix of countries is always important, so countries are added or dropped as political and economic conditions change. Recently, for instance, Haiti, Jordan, and South Africa were added, and service in Fiji, Botswana, and Tuvalu was discontinued. The Peace Corps also plans to open new programs in the next few months in Mozambique, Bangladesh, and the Georgian Republic.

Peace Corps volunteers themselves have changed some over the years as well. For many years, 60% or more of the volunteers were male; but that has not been true for several years, and, in fact, women now make up 54% of the volunteers.

One particularly exciting and very new feature of the Peace Corps is the Crisis Corps, an idea Gearan introduced. In the Crisis Corps, former Peace Corps volunteers are asked to serve for short periods of time during a crisis in a country with which they have considerable familiarity. This innovation was considered important enough for President Clinton to announce its inception from the Rose Garden. When there is a calamity such as a natural disaster or an intense food shortage, a group of experienced volunteers is put together to serve for a period of perhaps three to six months. In 1997, for example, eight volunteers served in the Czech Republic to help with flood relief. These people interrupted their lives and careers to return to a place where they were desperately needed and where they knew the "language, the people, and the culture. They were ready to begin work on day one."

The Peace Corps has inspired other countries to start similar organizations. Great Britain, Australia, New Zealand, Ireland, Canada, and Japan, among others, have volunteer organizations that are much like the Peace Corps. "The Peace Corps is now organizing that group and reaching out to other countries that want to start their own volunteer organizations." Mali, Senegal, and the Czech Republic are starting programs. Some nations wish to have a domestic corps, and others want an organization that will serve both inside and outside the country's borders. Helping other nations in every possible way with volunteer service work is "the ultimate legacy of the Peace Corps."

Although the immediate and primary mission of the Peace Corps is to serve other countries, there are many domestic dividends. "We've had more than 160,000 volunteers since 1961. They come back to our economy, which is increasingly global, and you have CEOs who want to hire Peace Corps volunteers. They've lived abroad and learned another language and culture," Gearan says. There is a National Peace Corps Association, which is quite active and has many loyal members. These people are organized into 120 groups around the country, both by geographical area of the United States and by country in which the members served. They do a great deal of volunteer work, and they always want briefings on international matters — "in-depth briefings on what's really going on, not the usual coverage." Gearan often travels to meet such groups and is no longer surprised to see "90 people turn out for a very early breakfast in Dayton, Ohio."

A large number of returning volunteers become teachers, and it's an impressive "domestic dividend to have teachers who are globally aware." Teachers College of Columbia University has a Peace Corps Fellows program in which returning volunteers work for a master's degree in education while teaching in an underserved area. The deans and prospective employers know that these people "have thought through what it means to serve in such areas, and they consider the volunteers excellent candidates." Surveys of volunteers show that Peace Corps alumni are more involved in community service and local volunteer work than is the typical American. "In addition to maintaining a keen interest in the Peace Corps, they get deeply involved in their communities, in schools, in churches, and in charitable institutions." Some enter public service or government. Donna Shalala, the secretary of health and human services; Sen. Christopher Dodd (D-Conn.); and five current members of the U.S. House of Representatives are former members of the Peace Corps.

I asked Mark Gearan what he would say to an audience of young people — say, high school students — about the Peace Corps. "Keep the Peace Corps in mind as you think about coursework and as you do volunteer activities such as tutoring." He further advises young people to stay in touch with the Peace Corps while in college — perhaps picking up Peace Corps literature or attending a meeting. But Gearan cautioned that the Peace Corps is not for everyone. "At the end of the day, you have to have a commitment to service to do this." It's a very important and fulfilling experience, but it's also 27 months of your life. You've really got to "want to make a difference in this particular way."

In his first radio address of 1998, President Clinton announced his intention to expand the Peace Corps by 50%. The goal is to increase the total number of volunteers serving around the world from 6,500 to 10,000 by the year 2000. No one questions the goals or the efficacy of the Peace Corps, but it must still compete for funds in a streamlined government. Gearan has consciously resolved "to spend a lot of time on our budget and our congressional relations — explaining to the Congress and our authorizers what we do with our money." He talks to any government official who will listen about the importance of the Peace Corps, drawing on his past experiences in government to guide him to the right people and to help him get in the door.

This is time-consuming work, much like the work Gearan has done in the past. He feels blessed to have "an involved spouse who is especially interested in and committed to public policy and government" and who herself has done this sort of work with its attendant long hours and travel. In fact, Gearan met his wife when they were co-workers on Father Drinan's 1978 campaign for Congress. Mary Gearan helps her husband see how easy it is to get bogged down in demanding bureaucratic work in Washington, which is not where the real value of the Peace Corps lies. To date, Gearan has visited volunteers in more than 20 countries. It's good to talk to office staff and members of Congress and federal officials responsible for Peace Corps authorizations, but "the best work is to go to a country where there are Peace Corps volunteers, get in a jeep, and go out to talk to volunteers where they are serving. That's the heart and soul of the Peace Corps," and that's where Mark Gearan gets reminded of what he learned as a young boy in Gardner, Massachusetts: "Government can be a force for good, and government can be a force to help others."

Shirley Strum Kenny

I always travel some distance (from Cambridge, Massachusetts, for Seymour Papert to Seattle for John Goodlad) to interview subjects — with one exception, President Kenny of the State University at Stony Brook, whose office is about three miles from my Long Island home. I knew that Kenny had chaired a national commission on undergraduate teaching and that the commission's report had just been issued. And, of course, she is a university president. When I learned the basic facts of her life during the time that I was considering her as a candidate for an interview, I made up my mind to write about her if she would allow it.

Kenny was born in East Texas during the Depression. This is a woman who figured out how to combine marriage, five children, a Ph.D., a career that included a full professorship, a department chair, a provost's position, two major university presidencies, chair of a prestigious national commission, and five books. At an age when many people are enjoying retirement and Medicare, Shirley Strum Kenny is talking about the next 10 years of work.

Now in her fourth year as president of the State University of New York at Stony Brook, after having served for nine years as president of Queens College of the City University of New York, Shirley Strum Kenny is passionate about the improvement of undergraduate education. In her inaugural address at Stony Brook in 1995 she proclaimed, "We will become the national model for undergraduate education at research universities. . . . We will find new ways to integrate the undergraduate experience with the research mission without compromising the research mission and without shortchanging the undergraduate experience." Excellence in undergraduate education became the first goal of the new

Originally published as "The Most Important Education in America: An Interview with Shirley Strum Kenny" in *Phi Delta Kappan* (March 1999). Used with permission.

president's five-year plan (1995-2000), which was developed by nine task forces composed of faculty members, students, alumni, community representatives, and staff members.

The capstone of Shirley Strum Kenny's commitment to improving undergraduate education is the report *Reinventing Undergraduate Education: A Blueprint for America's Research Universities*, which was produced by the Boyer Commission on Educating Undergraduates in the Research University. Funded by the Carnegie Foundation for the Advancement of Teaching, this national commission was chaired by Kenny. The commission's report is without question the preeminent document on reforming undergraduate education into the new millennium, and the interest in it has been remarkable. In the first two weeks after the report was issued in April 1998, the commission received nearly 20,000 "hits" on its website. There has been "enormous interest," according to Kenny, "including press interest. The interest is going well beyond research universities. Clearly, there have to be next steps."

Reinventing Undergraduate Education contains a chapter titled "Ten Ways to Change Undergraduate Education." When I asked Kenny which of the 10 were the most important, she immediately responded, "They're all key, but if you don't start with the freshman year, you've lost it." Of course, I asked her to illustrate from her first years at Stony Brook what could be done to improve freshman education. Many of the best teaching ideas and innovations for freshmen at Stony Brook have come from faculty members as a result of mini-grants that Kenny established for new teaching projects. The whole notion of incentives for improvement in teaching is important in a setting where "the faculty reward system has not always validated this effort." Innovation in teaching and particularly the personalization of education for entering students are now regular and important topics of conversation among Stony Brook faculty members.

At Stony Brook a form of block scheduling is becoming more common. This allows freshmen to "have three courses together, and the three professors teaching those courses work together. The students really get to know one another, and the teachers get to know the students." The university is beginning to establish "living/learning communities" in which the students live together as well as study together. Honors programs and other communities of students help overcome the anonymity that many students feel in a large, multifaceted university.

SUNY at Stony Brook has 18,000 students — 6,000 graduate students and 12,000 undergraduates. In addition, the complex includes a large teaching hospital and medical school, a Veterans' Administration Hospital, and a dental school. The university is also academically and legally connected to the nearby Brookhaven National Laboratory, a huge enterprise with 3,200 employees. President Kenny is the chairperson of Brookhaven Science Associates, the limited liability corporation that runs the laboratory. It is quite easy for a freshman to get lost in this powerful maze of academia, and therefore it is crucial to personalize the student's early experiences as much as possible.

While Stony Brook and most of the other 124 research universities in this country have made efforts to reform undergraduate education over the years, nothing has worked very well. Kenny thinks that the Boyer Commission report may have identified the reason: "The real problem is that we have assumed that good undergraduate education is what they do at small liberal arts colleges — and that's not who we are, and that kind of education never came to be a core value at research universities."

Places such as Ohio University and Princeton University, Rutgers and Harvard, Howard and UCLA need "scholar/teachers." Many universities already have undergraduates working with faculty members on research; more of that has to occur. "We can't think of students as empty vessels. We have got to teach them to frame their own questions, to find the information they need, to evaluate the information, to synthesize it, to come to conclusions, to solve the problem, and then to communicate the solution."

This is what scholars do, this is what comes naturally to them, and this is what they can inculcate in undergraduates. There is no longer a dichotomy between research and teaching. Without question, undergraduates must master a body of knowledge, and some of the traditional techniques are still valid. But scholar/ teachers must recognize "that there are also more interesting and effective ways of achieving mastery than the old-fashioned way."

Kenny understands that she and her contemporaries "learned in a linear fashion from books," while students today often learn from a screen that enables them to roam around to acquire new knowledge, a very different mental process. Kenny recognizes that learning and work in the modern world are "not disciplinary anywhere except in schools and universities, where we have these boxes called departments." In a world that has changed so much that some undergraduates are working with researchers closely enough to have written and presented papers with their mentors, the methods of teaching must change.

Some of the changes Kenny and the Boyer Commission promote are redirecting budgets to support interdisciplinary teaching, mentoring students, supporting inquiry-based learning in every possible way, linking strong oral and written experiences to every course, using technology creatively, and creating a community of learners. In short, "you have to begin with the concept of research as teaching, the concept of a student's right to research at a research university." The Boyer Commission report goes so far as to propose an Academic Bill of Rights for students that includes, among other things, the right "to learn through inquiry rather than the simple transmission of knowledge" and the right to receive training in "the skills necessary for oral and written communication" at a very high level.

All of this is quite far removed from the world in which Shirley Strum grew up in Texas just before, during, and after World War II. Born during the Great Depression in Tyler, a mid-sized town in East Texas not far from the Louisiana border, and educated in local schools, she learned early that she "loved school and that extraordinary teachers could make a difference in life." Two of her most memorable teachers were Miss Mitty Marsh in junior high school and Miss Sarah Marsh in high school, both English teachers. Particularly from the first Miss Marsh, Shirley Strum learned "the importance of rigor. I learned the importance of doing your work as nearly perfectly as you could, and that has stayed with me."

At the University of Texas, Austin, Kenny majored in English and journalism and served as editor of the school paper, the *Daily Texan*, in her senior year, taking over from Robert Kenny, who would soon become her husband. Once again, a great teacher — Leo Hughes — "engaged my imagination" and made Kenny want to study 18th century literature, the area that became her specialty and in which she published five books and many articles. She recalls how different learning and her attitude toward knowledge were in those days: "It was a much more limited world, and you really thought there was a set of knowledge to learn. People in Texas were just getting their first television sets."

The 20 years after her graduation from the University of Texas in 1955 were a time of cataclysmic change for both Kenny and the world. By the time she received her undergraduate degree, she knew that she wanted to make her career in academia. Her parents had never told her that there was anything she could not do; on the contrary, they had encouraged her to do whatever she wished. Between 1955 and 1975, she married Robert, lived in Louisiana with him while he served in the army, earned her M.A. from the University of Minnesota and a Ph.D. from the University of Chicago, published her first two books, had five children, and became a full professor at the University of Maryland.

Kenny's determination was so complete and the support and help from her husband, also an academic, was so unstinting that she hardly realized what it meant to be a woman in a male world. While she was working in the Folger Library in Washington, D.C., a colleague made a remark that opened her eyes. Kenny claimed that "she had never been discriminated against as a woman." The colleague responded, "That's because you were the pet woman, Shirley." She looked around and realized that most other women were still restricted to the lowest ranks and courses and that she was the rare woman who was being promoted.

Kenny soon became a department head and then a provost at the University of Maryland. "Once you get higher up in administration, you see that there are many people who are uncomfortable reporting to a woman. After they get to know you and you're Shirley, that changes. Also, there are incredible assumptions about you as a woman. Often people assumed I couldn't count." In fact, Kenny is excellent with numbers, likes mathematics, and is particularly good at budgets. Kenny was moving ahead at a time when both information and the role of women were changing in ways she could not have imagined just two decades earlier. She now understood that she hadn't gone into math "because I was a woman. I didn't become a doctor or lawyer because I had no notion I could become those things."

There was no sense of regret when Kenny made these remarks to me. In fact, many of the skills that she might have used in mathematics, law, or medicine she uses in her daily work — not to mention that she is the president of a university that includes a medical school. She understands that she also gets to use her mother's skills of patient listening and thoughtful questioning, examples of which she saw during the civil rights movement in the South when her mother helped local people understand what was happening and what should happen. Kenny is proud to have inherited her father's speed with numbers and his mix of shrewdness, kindness, and fun in his business — a chain of high-fashion shoe stores that he founded and ran for many years in Texas, Louisiana, and Arkansas.

Business sense has become increasingly important to Kenny. "I've really learned to take a more corporate approach to university administration. When I look at the budget, I look at it as an organism that may need pruning to do some other things better. For example, I eliminated layers of administration; as a result, the bureaucracy works better and faster. I learned to think about what your core products and values are and what you want to grow." Stony Brook has nearly 10,000 employees in addition to Brookhaven National Laboratory's 3,200, so the budget, grants, and resources are very substantial and must be regarded in both a human and businesslike way.

Kenny serves as a board member of two large corporations, Toys "R" Us and Computer Associates. Charles Lazarus, CEO of

Toys "R" Us, and Charles Wang, CEO of Computer Associates, are important influences on her. Both men have a way of looking at their enterprises that allows them not only to see possible areas of growth but also, like Kenny's father, to have fun doing business.

While the demands of running a large institution prevent Kenny from having the pleasure of teaching a class or following through herself on an interesting new teaching idea, the presidency does give her the opportunity to set interesting things in motion or to support good programs that predated her arrival. She recalls that when she was chairperson of the English Department at the University of Maryland, she proposed a Renaissance and Baroque Studies Center for the university. When she became provost, she approved that plan. "I saw that it was a lot easier to get things done if you had influence."

At Stony Brook, Kenny supports such efforts as the Center for Innovation and Excellence (CIE) and Women in Science and Engineering (WISE). She was able to reach out to a friend, Dennis Mehiel, the founder and owner of the Four M Company, to sponsor a program called All the Way. This program, now in its third year, will serve 360 minority students at P.S. 132 in New York City over a 12-year period. The children will be followed through junior and senior high school and will receive many forms of help and support from the university, such as services from the School of Social Work, mentoring, after-school programs, free medical care, and field trips to the university. Upon high school graduation, each qualified participant "will have the opportunity to attend SUNY at Stony Brook tuition-free."

SUNY at Stony Brook celebrated its 40th anniversary in 1997. In the "most recent National Research Council rankings, Stony Brook had nine programs in the top quartile of graduate programs in the country." In the Graham-Diamond study published by the Johns Hopkins University Press, Stony Brook was recognized as one of the nation's top three public research universities based on faculty members' per-capita research productivity, along with Berkeley and the Santa Barbara campus of the University of California system. Among all research universities, Stony Brook ranked 11th, surpassed only by such institutions as Stanford, Harvard, Princeton, and Yale. There will soon be a major new building on the campus, a $25 million cross-cultural, high-technology Asian American Center donated by Charles Wang. Stony Brook already has a Nobel laureate, four MacArthur Foundation fellows, more than 2,000 sponsored projects, and more than $100 million in external research support.

Virtually all of Shirley Strum Kenny's own education and career have been spent in public institutions, from elementary school to college at the University of Texas to service at the University of Maryland, Queens College, and now SUNY at Stony Brook. "My commitment has always been to public higher education. I believe that's the most important education in America. That is where you get the energy from people who have their one chance. They're not choosing from among private schools. This is it, and that's what I resonate to."

Dorothy Rich

Dorothy Rich was an easy person to interview and to like: feisty, engaging, bright, and animated. I quickly formed the opinion that Dorothy could charm me or curse me out — or anything in between. I had a much more difficult time warming to her work. This was not Madeline Hunter focusing with laser-like intelligence and precision on a difficult body of theoretical work and transforming it into practice. This was not Ernie Boyer grappling with the largest questions of purpose or ethics in education.

As the interview progressed, the accumulation of what Dorothy Rich had done began to capture me. Dr. Rich had invented no new method or theory, nor had she done any original research. What she had done was to accumulate over three decades the most ordinary things any parent or teacher could do to help a child get ready to learn and to organize her collection of, literally, thousands of activities and ideas into categories that hundreds of thousands of parents and teachers have found helpful. Using boxes and lamps and pencils and string and cars and other items of everyday life, Rich has created an impressive foundation for learning.

An energetic, bright, determined, and plainspoken woman, Dorothy Rich took the obvious and the mundane and transformed them into a well-organized educational enterprise. Everyone in education knows how crucial the family is to a child's educational success, but rarely do educators do more than bemoan the fact that a particular child is ill-prepared to learn. During the 1960s and 1970s, when the continuing calls for school reform began to sweep the profession as a result of books by such people as John

Originally published as "Recipes for School Success: An Interview with Dorothy Rich" in *Phi Delta Kappan* (June 1999). Used with permission.

Holt, Christopher Jencks, and Jonathan Kozol, it was the rare educator who thought to put together the hundreds of ways in which parents could be of specific help to children in their homes. Almost all the reform and support programs then and since — such as Head Start or programs to train teachers and administrators to do things differently in the school — have concentrated on offering help outside the home.

But Dorothy Rich took a different approach. Using paper cartons, tables, lamps, chairs, electric bills, and other paraphernalia of daily life in a home, Rich began in the early 1960s to construct "recipes" and to generate modest ideas that would teach parents how to help their children learn what they needed to know to achieve academic success. She began offering workshops to parents, teachers, administrators, guidance counselors, and other school professionals. Rich's original purposes were to teach parents the homespun methods they could use to help their children get ready for success in school and to show educators how they could help parents use these methods. It soon became apparent to Rich that selected parents and school personnel could train other groups.

Dorothy Rich's recipes for school success became known to many community and education organizations in the 1970s, particularly in the Washington, D.C., area where Rich lived. Michael Casserly, executive director of the Council of the Great City Schools, lauds Rich as one of a handful of people who understood early on the important role families could play and who eventually influenced the parent involvement component of the federal Title I program. Rich now works with the U.S. Department of Education on ways in which parents can be part of any improvement or reform program.

The Home and School Institute — incorporated as a not-for-profit organization in Washington, D.C., in 1972 with Dorothy Rich as its president — has to date trained more than 100,000 families in 48 states in the art of using egg cartons, empty boxes, the monthly rent or mortgage bills, vacuum cleaners, and cars to help children both at home and in school to get ready to learn.

Rich's book *MegaSkills*, first published by Houghton Mifflin in 1988, organizes many of her ideas and specific lessons and is now in its third edition with more than 35,000 copies sold. The book has been endorsed by Marian Wright Edelman, president of the Children's Defense Fund; by Robert Chase, president of the National Education Association; by Tipper Gore; and by former senator and now Presidential candidate Bill Bradley. This is heady stuff for a woman raised in a modest home in Michigan where "chickens roamed in the backyard."

Dorothy Rich grew up as the child of immigrant parents in the 1930s and early 1940s in Monroe, Michigan. "Mine is the first generation in my family to go to college," she relates. In fact, her parents were never comfortable with English and spoke Yiddish at home. But they did emphasize the extreme importance of education to Dorothy and her brother, both of whom eventually earned doctorates, and they did everything they could to encourage their children to do well in the "solid, excellent, supportive schools in Monroe, where teachers really cared about you and taught with purpose."

When Dorothy was 13, her mother died after a two-year illness, and the family moved to Detroit. Her older brother went to college, and Dorothy found herself an outsider in the city high school, "which was too big and where it was difficult for a teenager to break in socially if you didn't know people from the earlier years." In spite of that, Dorothy did well in her schoolwork, went to the University of Michigan for two years, and completed her undergraduate work at Wayne State University. By 1964 she had earned a master's degree from Teachers College, Columbia University; had taught in two schools in different states; had married and moved to Washington, D.C.; and was the at-home mother of two small children. As a result of what she had learned in the previous few years at Teachers College and as a high school teacher in Virginia, she began conducting workshops for teachers and parents in the evening division of the University of Virginia.

When Rich taught high school in Virginia in the late 1950s and asked her colleagues in several grades why so many youngsters did not seem prepared to learn, she got a standard answer. "My high school colleagues said the junior high teachers didn't do the job; the junior high teachers blamed the elementary teachers, who in turn blamed the family. So I began to ask, What do we want the family to do?" Motherhood gave her considerable insight into just how rapidly and how much children could learn at home. In the professional literature, she was influenced by the work of Benjamin Bloom, who had "started to measure what children learn before they come to school. Bloom was interested in the role of the family — something that was never mentioned in any teacher-training work." Rich soon became convinced that there were skills that children needed to learn outside of school if they were going to do well in school subjects.

In 1964 Rich began a Sunday column in the *Washington Post* called "Home and School." Each week, she wrote about specific ways in which families could help children prepare for school. "This was before the time of self-help books and included recipes for promoting learning in English, social studies, mathematics, and other school subjects." The recipes began to pile up, Rich began to have a serious readership, and she was now conducting more fully developed workshops for parents, called "Success for Children Begins at Home."

By 1972, when Rich established the Home and School Institute, she had hundreds of recipes for learning that began to form around such concepts as confidence and responsibility — concepts that would eventually become what Rich calls MegaSkills. The University of Virginia's Northern Virginia Center, Trinity College, and Catholic University began to support Rich's work. In addition, "I had a considerable following from the *Washington Post* column, and school districts would often give me a room where I could do training. Sometimes the schools paid for this, and sometimes parents paid."

In 1980 the U.S. Department of Education asked Rich to develop a program for special education. She "took rooms in two schools in Washington and turned them into a replica of a home. Throughout this home I attached special education home-learning recipes to walls, furniture, and lamps. The children would come in with their parents, and we would demonstrate how this works. It was called The Family Place, and I trained teachers and paraprofessionals to do the training." Rich's program kept expanding into areas such as bilingual training or training that concentrated on the specific needs of the American Postal Workers' Union or the American Red Cross or Parents Without Partners.

By 1987 Rich was able to "pull together my work from many previous years and programs" and develop it into an organized program with application to all groups interested in education — but there was no book to illustrate her accomplishment.

Rich had received support from the Mott Foundation and the John D. and Catherine T. MacArthur Foundation. She had also taken the program around the country and had prepared several of the best participants in her program to become trainers. In addition, Rich had received her doctorate from Catholic University, where her work focused on the relationship between home learning and school achievement. Her doctoral work, of course, got her to think more seriously about organizing her lessons, recipes, and training programs more carefully and coherently. Just at that point, Don Cameron of the National Education Association, where Rich rented office space, saw the piles of booklets and pamphlets and materials all over her office and told her, "You're the Dr. Spock of education, Dorothy, but not enough people know about you. You've got to pull all this together in a book." Cameron's persistent encouragement was the impetus for Rich to write *MegaSkills*.

"The MegaSkills are the values, the attitudes, and the behaviors that determine success in school and on the job," she states. Over a period of years, the skills that emerged were Confidence, Motivation, Effort, Responsibility, Initiative, Perseverance, Caring, Teamwork, Common Sense, Problem Solving, and Focus. And it was around these 11 MegaSkills that Rich organized her book. There are dozens of recipes to go with each skill, and new recipes are developed each year. "If I'm going to teach a youngster responsibility, for instance, one recipe is called 'My Special

Place.' The special place is a simple box at the front door. This is where the child, assisted by a parent if necessary, places everything he or she will need for school in the morning." The telephone is an excellent tool for teaching Confidence. "With a very young child, we do activities that help the child to get confident about dialing numbers, dialing grandma, reading left to right. With an older child, we use the telephone to get information. When does the movie start, or when does the library close?"

MegaSkills is not designed to substitute for the work of school, although the program does link recipes to academic objectives. Looking at a mortgage statement or an insurance policy with a youngster is linked to mathematics and reading. Pointing out natural objects while walking down an ordinary street with a child links to science. Nothing in the MegaSkills program is extremely complex or demanding. That sort of work is left for school. This is basic preparation for success, and Rich is the first to acknowledge that her program is "not rocket science." What is rocket science about her program, however, is its organization into 11 categories, the hundreds and hundreds of elegantly simple and well-conceived recipes to support the categories, and the many applications for the MegaSkills. No parent or teacher or group of parents and teachers could easily put together what more than 30 years of careful thought, accumulation of successful lessons, and field-testing have created.

MegaSkills is a brand name for the recipes it represents. But it is also a proven and serious training program. "If you're going to call it MegaSkills, you must use the MegaSkills training activities, and you don't just put in positive parenting or some other material that may be respectable but is not part of this program. This is not a management program of children; it is not a discipline program; it's a program designed to build academics and character development in young people — basically the habits and attitudes and behaviors you need for learning and ultimately for job success." The focus is on using the home to supplement what the school does, not to supplant it. The parents or the professionals who are going to train the parents go through a fully configured workshop that includes warm-up activities, demonstrations, lectures, and small-group activities. There is considerable room for creativity on the part of the workshop leader in how things are presented, but the broad outline and most of the activities are provided.

All the publicity for MegaSkills is by word of mouth. From Saipan to Alaska, from New York to Nebraska, MegaSkills workshops are held because some community group or school has requested a session. Usually there are 24 people taking part in a one- or two-day workshop, though longer workshops can be provided. The cost of the workshops includes all of the books and materials that are needed for the session as well as any follow-up meetings. There are eight qualified trainers and 1,500 certified workshop leaders who have taught MegaSkills workshops in four countries and 48 states. These are all experienced people who have come through the ranks of the organization. The leaders work with Rich, are highly qualified, and do all the original training of a group. The trainers are some of the best people who have gone through workshops and in turn train people in their local areas. In fact, MegaSkills training stresses the obligation to share what you have learned with others. Altogether, these leaders have appeared in 3,000 schools in the United States.

Dorothy Rich's work has been recognized and honored in many ways. She has received citations for the excellence and usefulness of her work from the National Governors' Association and the U.S. Department of Education. In 1992 the MegaSkills program received the A+ for Breaking the Mold Award from the U.S. Department of Education after several school districts reported good results. In Memphis, for example, researchers from Memphis State University reported that MegaSkills students were watching less TV than other students. Research specialists from the schools in Austin reported that students exposed to MegaSkills got better scores on national and state achievement tests and had fewer discipline problems in school than did other students.

None of this completely satisfies Dorothy Rich. She wants entire schools to be organized around MegaSkills. Indeed, she even has a visionary plan for a MegaSkills city. Rich is certain that youngsters today are less prepared to learn than they were 25 years ago. "MegaSkills can give students a structured program to move through the mess and endless complexity of learning. Just because a teacher says something to a student doesn't mean the student has absorbed or learned it." Students need the basic supporting structures to be able to focus on learning: the 11 skills that enable all important learning in school and in work. Rich is equally convinced that many adults also are lacking in MegaSkills and can't be proper role models for young people. In her characteristically energetic and creative way, Dorothy Rich continually thinks of new audiences, new recipes, new training ideas, and new ways to get people to pay attention to the MegaSkills program. She has decided that, instead of putting "children first, I now believe it's parents and teachers first. We have to teach them MegaSkills, so they can be proper role models, and so they can teach those skills to children."

Manuel Justiz

As I usually do for interviews, I arrived early at the University of Texas campus where I was scheduled to meet Dean Manuel Justiz in his College of Education office. The campus publicity states there are more than 50,000 students and 12,000 employees on the 357-acre Austin campus, and I believe it after wading through the crowd when, I assume, many classes were changing. It was like walking on a crowded street in New York City. Cars moved very slowly and gingerly down the main street that bisects the campus, and people were five or six abreast on the sidewalk. Dean Justiz later told me that one dormitory is so large it has its own zip code.

Experiencing the density and size of the campus in a morning walk helped me to understand the political importance of this place in Texas. This is the main campus of Texas' state university, directly across town from the state capitol, the governor's mansion, and several government offices, a campus rich in tradition from the prominence of its business school to the success of its sports teams. The Lyndon B. Johnson Library is on this campus, and it was to this campus and its College of Education that the Texas legislature looked for the recent support it got in its deliberations on standards, testing and teacher training.

On 21 January 1961, 12-year-old Manuel Justiz and his 9-year-old sister Maria left Communist Cuba on a so-called Peter Pan flight to freedom, under the aegis of Catholic Welfare. The Castro government had agreed to allow the Justiz children to leave the country but had ruled that their parents, both educated professionals, had to remain — even though they did not agree with the government's policies. The parents made the difficult decision to

Originally published as "Making a Difference Through Education: An Interview with Manuel Justiz" in *Phi Delta Kappan* (December 1999). Used with permission.

send their children to freedom alone because, otherwise, their son was scheduled to be sent to Red China in a few months for "militia training."

When Manuel and Maria arrived in Miami, Manuel wore a name tag that his father had made for him: "My name is Manuel Justiz. I'm a Cuban refugee. I do not speak English, and I do not have any family." Manuel and Maria were sent to live with a foster family in Albuquerque, New Mexico, and they did not know whether their mother and father were alive or dead until their parents escaped from Cuba more than four years later.

In October 1982, 21 years after arriving as a refugee, Manuel Justiz was recommended to the U.S. Senate by President Reagan for appointment as director of the National Institute of Education (NIE), the research division of the U.S. Department of Education. At that time, the NIE had a staff of 249 people, 155 of whom (like Justiz) held doctoral degrees. When his nomination was approved, Manuel Justiz became "the youngest director in the history of the agency, the first Hispanic director, the first director who came from west of the Mississippi, and the first director who had not graduated from an Ivy League institution." Today, Justiz is dean of the College of Education at the University of Texas, Austin, and holder of both the Lee Hage Jamail Regents Chair in Education and the A.M. Aikin Regents Chair in Education Leadership.

But his early years in the U.S. did not predict such high achievement. Late in 1961, young Manny and Maria were placed with a family in New Mexico that did not speak Spanish. Their adjustment to a new country and to an area in which there were few other Cubans was difficult. When their parents arrived in the United States more than four years later, the family reunited and moved to Emporia, Kansas, where the federal government had a program to retrain highly educated adult Cuban refugees as teachers. Manny graduated from high school in Emporia and completed both his B.A. and M.S. degrees at nearby Emporia State University.

In 1973 Justiz accepted a position at Haskell Indian Junior College in Lawrence, Kansas, the first of several positions that would introduce him to the complexities of American culture. "That gave me an opportunity to appreciate and understand the richness and diversity of American Indian culture and the differences in tribes across the country."

Over the next eight years — 1974 to 1982 — Justiz completed a doctorate in higher education at Southern Illinois University, gained broad experience reviewing grant proposals and developing research programs for Hispanics and American Indians for the Lilly Endowment, and worked in Latin American and multicultural programs at the University of New Mexico. His work there took him to virtually every Latin American country and put him in contact with World Bank and USAID staff, as well as with many ministers of education in Latin American countries and with education liaison officials in U.S. embassies.

By the time Justiz arrived in Washington, D.C., he was well-versed in American and Latin American education, had acquaintances in many ethnic and cultural groups in the hemisphere, and had accumulated considerable expertise in education research and issues affecting the public schools and higher education. Of course, he was not yet skilled in the ways of Washington politics.

Fortunately for him, then-Secretary of Education Terrel (Ted) Bell "became a great friend and mentor" in an atmosphere in which many ultra-conservative politicians were calling for the abolition of the Department of Education and the NIE. "Ted had the savvy and the courage to shift the debate to issues of great concern to the public and to policy makers and away from the political tensions" that swirled outside the walls of the department. Justiz was able to play an important advisory role in the formulation of *A Nation at Risk*, without a doubt the most influential document on education published by the federal government during the 1980s.

Released by the Bell-appointed National Commission on Excellence in Education in April 1983, *A Nation at Risk* was one of the first modern documents to bring "great recognition to the whole issue of standards." Though short — only 33 pages in length — the report used direct language to warn of a "threat from within": declining education standards that "could lead to serious economic consequences" for the United States. *A Nation at Risk* held a prominent position in the national news for weeks, and it opened a serious debate about what was going on in U.S. public schools.

In 1984 Justiz appointed a study group to take a look at higher education. In 1985 that group issued a report, *Involvement in Learning*, which called for "greater student involvement in the learning process" and which recommended "that institutions of higher education establish higher standards for student achievement."

Justiz spent the next few years — 1985 to 1989 — in a more reflective setting as a chaired professor of education at the University of South Carolina. During that interval, he served as senior and contributing editor of two books, *Higher Education Research and Public Policy* and *Minorities in Education*, both of them published by the American Council on Education/Macmillan Publishing Company. During those years, Justiz also wrote a number of articles reflecting on his time in Washington and clarifying his position on important education issues. In late 1989, he was invited to become dean of the College of Education at the University of Texas, Austin, a post he assumed on 1 January 1990.

Though he believes in being "gracious and cooperative," Justiz has clearly marked himself as a maverick among education deans. He is far more interested in working directly with the public schools, with other divisions within the university, with policy makers, and with the business community than with either professional education organizations or other colleges of education. In his view, too many educators have a "circle-the-wagons" attitude toward legislators and policy makers. Justiz has made it his goal to reach out and build a strong relationship with the business community and with policy leaders in Texas. In fact, when the Texas legislature restricted the role of schools of education in training teachers, he sided with the legislature and opposed the National Council for Accreditation of Teacher Education (NCATE).

Manny Justiz was firm about wanting the College of Education to be a partner with other colleges at the University of Texas and a real player in Texas education. When NCATE eventually called for the condemnation of the Texas legislature, Justiz canceled the school's NCATE membership, saying, "Our goal is to be the place that the people of Texas look to for understanding the problems of education in the state of Texas and for coming up with solutions to those problems. If we have to choose, we will choose the Texas legislature and the people of Texas before we choose a professional organization."

In essence, the conflict was over emphasizing training in content (for example, mathematics, chemistry, English) versus emphasizing training in methods of teaching and in the history and philosophy of education. Though determined to have his college continue to play a strong role in teacher preparation and education research, Justiz clearly came down on the side of focusing on content in the training of prospective teachers.

Now completing his 10th year as dean, Justiz continues to work closely with the Texas business community, the local schools, the governor's business council, and various colleges at the University of Texas (for example, business, natural sciences) to improve the College of Education. When Gov. George W. Bush made reading a priority for his administration, "We responded by competing for and receiving an award for the Texas Center for Reading and Language Arts. Three years later, we have one of the leading reading centers in the country. We regard this as an opportunity to do what is right for the children of Texas and to respond to a call from the governor." The center has established two primary goals: "helping schools throughout the state to make sure that every child reads on grade level by the third grade and stays on grade level thereafter" and providing coursework to ensure that every teacher graduate "is a reading teacher with appropriate knowledge of the converging research base on beginning reading."

Meanwhile, the College of Education has a strong partnership with the Graduate School of Business to train business leaders in human resource development. It also has a strong partnership with the College of Natural Sciences to train secondary teachers of science and mathematics. "They provide the content, and we provide the skills of teaching that content — finding effective ways of communicating that content to students." The program with the College of Natural Sciences was recently the focus of a site visit from the National Science Foundation (NSF). The hope is that the University of Texas will become a major center for the teaching of math and science. The NSF realizes that there are not many formal partnerships at major research universities like that between the University of Texas College of Education and its College of Natural Sciences.

Repeatedly over the past few years, the College of Education has shown itself to be highly responsive to the Texas business community. Indeed, the college has been complimented more than once by the governor and by the Board of Regents for its responsiveness to problems that the business community or the government sees in education. Justiz emphasized especially the college's willingness to work with the Texas Education Agency, with the governor's education advisor, and with the governor's business council both on establishing standards for teachers and students and on solving real-world problems in Texas schools.

The serious commitment of the College of Education to Texas schools is best illustrated by its relationships with the schools in Austin and Dallas. More than 60% of all University of Texas teacher graduates go to work for the Austin Independent School District, so the college's relationship with the local school district is natural, close, and strong. Recently, Justiz and several Austin Independent School District administrators interviewed a number of recent graduates. Two questions that were posed were, What did we do well to prepare you to teach? What could we have done better? A committee of teachers, principals, and university faculty members used the results of that survey to bring about changes in the teacher preparation program, including the addition of a new requirement related to the uses of technology. When Austin school administrators hire an education graduate from the University of Texas these days, they get a new teacher who exceeds the education technology requirements established for employment in the district.

Meanwhile, in Dallas, the College of Education operates a fast-track program to prepare new principals. Faculty members in the Department of Educational Administration work with district representatives to identify outstanding teachers who hope to become principals, and those candidates spend one summer in residence at the Austin campus. During the following year, UT faculty members go to Dallas to teach courses. Candidates then spend a second summer in residence at UT, followed by a one-year clinical internship. At the end of the second year, successful candidates receive a master's degree and certification as a principal.

In both of the examples above, "the concept is one of a College of Education that rolls up its sleeves and works in partnership with a school district. We cannot afford to be in the ivory tower simply writing about the issues." Rather, Justiz believes that he and his faculty must be present in the schools, experiencing real problems and helping with real solutions.

Each professional staff member in the College of Education is strongly encouraged to work in the schools, and such work is noted in each faculty member's annual review and reflected in merit salary increases. College of Education faculty members have embraced this challenge, recognizing that, "to prepare teachers, one has to understand the classrooms of today, the complexities of learning, changes in the family unit, the diversity of the student population, and all the other problems and challenges that exist in today's schools."

Faculty members respond to the challenge in a variety of ways, depending on their strengths, interests, and talents. They may work with teachers and administrators on reading instruction, meeting standards, cooperative learning, leadership, staff development, or any other area in which a school has a need and a faculty member has expertise and interest. Justiz visits public school students and faculty members frequently to gauge how well his College of Education is preparing teachers for the classrooms they enter. When he discovered that most UT education majors did their student teaching in high-performing classrooms but were then hired to work in low-performing classrooms, he pushed for changes that placed a larger number of student teachers where the jobs were.

Justiz stated more than once that he was fortunate to "inherit a rich environment" when he came to the University of Texas. The College of Education is "a very high-performing organization with a lot of good people working together on a shared philosophy" characterized by broad common goals: putting the people of Texas ahead of any education organization, engaging in serious scholarship and research while simultaneously contributing to the real world of schools, and working as a team to solve problems. "We were the first college in the state to break ranks with the education establishment — and the first major school of education in the country to say, 'We will not be a party to education politics; we will side with our own legislature and hold firm to the belief that teacher training is a universitywide responsibility that we have one important piece of'."

The Justiz family is an American success story. Manny Justiz' parents did retrain as teachers in the government program in Emporia, Kansas, and his mother — now 75 years of age — still teaches Spanish at El Dorado High School in Albuquerque. Justiz' father, who had been a lawyer in Cuba, died several years ago, but he had a long second career as a professor of Spanish at a community college. As for Maria, she is a special education teacher.

When I asked Manny Justiz why he chose education over law or business or some other profession, he responded, "Choosing a career in education gave me the chance to pay back this great nation for the freedoms and opportunities I received here as a young boy and man. I developed a great passion for education, and I treasured the knowledge that education is the one thing I have that can never be taken from me. That knowledge gave me the confidence that I could make a difference — through education — for others, as well."

Hugh Price

Each person prepared differently for his or her interview. Some people provided me with a great deal of background information (Dorothy Rich), and other people simply relied on me to ask very specific questions (Stephen Jay Gould). While Hugh Price answered every question I put to him with as much detail as I required, he also was extremely well prepared for the interview.

Mr. Price had a television and VCR set up, so I could see what some of the events in the Urban League's youth achievement effort looked like. He provided me with a book of press clippings and made sure I noticed several that were very important to him. In addition, both Mr. Price and his administrative assistant, Juliet Warner Joseph, gave me several National Urban League publications; during the interview, Price glanced at some notes on a hassock in front of him, so that nothing of great importance would fail to be in the interview. As always, I relied mostly on the audiotape I made of the interview, but I was able to check facts and gain a somewhat deeper appreciation of Hugh Price's work at the National Urban League as a result of his excellent preparation.

Hugh Price has been president and chief executive officer of the National Urban League since 1 July 1994. Founded in 1910, the National Urban League is "the premier social service and civil rights organization in America." The organization occupies two handsomely decorated floors in a historic building at the foot of New York City's Wall Street, overlooking the East River. There are also 114 affiliate offices in 34 states.

The National Urban League has a great deal on its plate — issues ranging from the profiling of African Americans by police for criminal investigation and the controversy surrounding the

Originally published as "Committed to High-Quality Education for All Children: An Interview with Hugh Price" in *Phi Delta Kappan* (April 2000). Used with permission.

February 1999 killing of Amadou Diallo, an unarmed and inno-
cent black man in New York City, to helping African Americans
gain economic power through equalization of earnings, investment in stocks, and home ownership. However, in the past two
years education — always a fundamental concern for the Urban
League — has in many ways become the centerpiece of the organization's effort "to assist African Americans in the achievement
of social and economic equality."

The motto (almost a mantra) "Our Children = Our Destiny" is
displayed on the wall of the Urban League's headquarters and in
Urban League publications, leaving no doubt that young people
are the primary focus of this organization. In several public statements he has made since 1997, Price has reiterated a set of rights
for "every child in America." First, each child has the right to a
high-quality preschool education. Second, all children should
have highly qualified teachers who believe that they can learn.
Third, all children should have access to challenging courses of
study. Fourth, schools and communities should be organized for
learning and not just for maintaining order. And finally, schools
should provide high-quality academic and social programs after
school and in the summer that keep children out of harm's way.

Under Price's leadership, the National Urban League — working in concert with the Congress of National Black Churches,
black sororities and fraternities, and some 25 other African-
American organizations — fleshed out these rights by initiating,
in August 1997, a major campaign for recognition of educational
achievement by African Americans. For example, a black national honor society, the Thurgood Marshall Achievers Society, was
established, and in the spring of 1998 it inducted the first 4,000
young African Americans in ceremonies held in 36 black churches
across the country. Gen. Colin Powell addressed one group of
young achievers in the Metropolitan Baptist Church in Washington, D.C., as part of the Urban League's effort to "spread the
gospel that achievement matters."

Another important effort aims to make young African Americans aware of the importance of the SAT and of what they must

do to score well on that examination. "September has been established as Achievement Month," Price points out, "and on the third Saturday in September events are held all over the country." In 1998, 40,000 black youngsters participated. In Columbia, South Carolina, for example, 700 black students and their parents showed up for an SAT Awareness Assembly sponsored by the local affiliate, the Columbia Urban League, which took place in the chapel at Benedict College. The 700 youngsters heard again and again that "achievement matters" and that they control their own destiny through their academic efforts; they also received information and resources that would help them prepare for the SAT. Performance on that college admissions examination and all other forms of academic accomplishment are very important to Price, who cites one study on urban education showing that "the vast majority of black boys scarcely care about achievement by the time they hit high school."

Solving the problem of poor academic achievement among black students, particularly in the inner cities, is a complex undertaking that will take time. The National Urban League recognizes the need to work on several fronts simultaneously. One important task is to identify parents and organizations able to evaluate the local schools to determine whether they are doing everything possible to offer a high-quality education. Working through black churches and other large black organizations is very helpful. However, the push to stimulate black academic achievement must extend even more deeply into the black community. "People are not islands. They're invariably connected to something, and we've got to find that something," Price insists. There are organizations of barbers and beauticians, storefront churches, block associations, and dozens of other groups that together embrace most members of any African-American community.

Information that will stimulate local consumer demand for better schools and higher achievement can be discovered and disseminated in a variety of ways. The National Urban League sponsors "local education summits to educate black parents about the achievement gap and to teach them how to improve local education." To be effective, Price points out, parents must collect data on an individual school, not "aggregate data for the entire school district." They must learn, for instance, whether the teachers are certified in the subjects they teach and whether most students are taking challenging courses. The National Urban League prepares and publicizes position papers on education policy, and Price himself speaks to editorial boards and organizations across the country, relentlessly "pushing the message that achievement matters."

The State Farm Life Insurance Company has provided funding to publicize that message. Ads are placed in newspapers and journals that are read by African Americans, and billboards in black communities remind local residents that "achievement matters."

Meanwhile, the Lilly Endowment has given the National Urban League $25 million to fund achievement campaigns orchestrated by local affiliates and to fund college scholarships for minority youngsters who have performed well academically. That sum, to be used over a five-year period, is the largest single foundation gift in the National Urban League's history.

The National Urban League commissioned Linda Darling-Hammond, Charles E. Ducommon Professor of Teaching and Teacher Education at Stanford University, to write an article for the League's 1998 publication, *The State of Black America*. Among other findings, Darling-Hammond determined that, while black students are held to the same high standards as other children, too frequently the schools that serve them lack teachers who are certified in math and science, pay their teachers less well than those in the suburbs are paid, lack motivated teachers who believe that all children can learn, and house children in very large and impersonal buildings. Price asks, "How can states hold children responsible for higher standards with a straight face if they can't guarantee the higher-quality education that must go with those standards? You must ask whether children are being offered the high-quality education that enables them to meet high standards."

Hugh Price was not himself a child of poverty, although much of his life story reflects the history of the black community since

World War II. His father was a physician in Washington, D.C., who had both a private practice and a position on the medical faculty at Howard University. His mother was a housewife and a career volunteer who worked with Americans for Democratic Action and played a role in the effort to bring the vote to the District of Columbia.

Born in 1941, young Hugh spent his first six school years attending segregated schools in Washington. In 1953, when he was in the seventh grade, his parents moved him to Georgetown Day School, where "many people fighting for integration sent their children." Price's parents "were part of a group of people who helped finance some of the early cases opposing school segregation that were brought by the NAACP [National Association for the Advancement of Colored People] Legal Defense and Educational Fund."

In 1954, Hugh Price was a member of the first group of black students to integrate the schools of Washington, D.C. He recalls protests by white students at Taft Junior High School and — later — being "very lonely" at Calvin Coolidge High School, where he was one of a small group of African-American students. In 1959, Price enrolled at Amherst College, where he was one of five black students in a class of 250. He and two other African Americans graduated in 1963; and he went on to Yale Law School, from which he graduated in 1966. Price met the woman who would become his wife during his first year of college. She was the only black student at Mt. Holyoke College in 1959-60.

While attending Yale Law School, Price worked as a "social-group worker with six teenagers in the New Haven antipoverty program." That was his introduction to formal youth development, which became an abiding interest and a theme that has marked much of his subsequent career. After completing law school, Price worked briefly as a neighborhood attorney with the New Haven Legal Assistance Association. He then worked with an urban affairs consulting firm and later served as human resources administrator for the city of New Haven. From 1978 to 1982, Price served on the editorial board of the *New York Times*, often writing about education and urban policy. In 1982 he became senior vice president of WNET/Thirteen, the nation's largest public television station, and in 1988 he became vice president of the Rockefeller Foundation.

At Rockefeller, Price played a leading role in conceiving and launching such education initiatives as the National Commission on Teaching and America's Future, the Coalition of Community Foundations for Youth, the Learning Communities Network, and the National Guard Youth ChalleNGe Corps, all "programs designed to close the gap that separates minorities from the rest of society or to assist with school reform."

The ChalleNGe Corps is a program that Price views with great pride. "It operates in more than two dozen states and has become the most powerful intervention I know of for young people who have dropped out of school." Its participants are young people in considerable turmoil, having failed in and been failed by their schools. The ChalleNGe Corps currently boasts of a 73% completion rate for the GED (General Education Development) diploma, a retention rate of about 90% of enrollees, and very high placement rates for graduates. "The core idea is to take the youngsters to a military base, keep them around the clock, get them ramped up to pass the GED, and teach them the skills of both leadership and followership." Young people learn to work with customers and bosses; they also learn how to exercise initiative and leadership. When these students leave the Corps, they are assigned to mentors who can advise them and encourage them to continue their education in a two- or four-year college.

It was his experience with the Youth ChalleNGe Corps that convinced Price of the value of having the National Urban League embark on a massive education initiative. He knows that urban minority youngsters can flourish in a variety of settings. There is some evidence, he notes, that many black children thrive best in smaller school settings where they can learn in small groups from teachers who know them well. The ChalleNGe Corps illustrates that, "if we can be flexible in our approach and try to place youngsters in settings that give them a maximum shot at success, we can pull many more of them through than we might otherwise have been able to do."

Price and the National Urban League not only favor charter schools but also openly promote them as long as they are publicly financed and accountable to the public. In fact, the street academies originated by the Urban League in the 1960s, which were called "alternative schools," were among the first charter-like schools in the country. "We are supportive of the idea of charter schools because we know that one size does not fit all youngsters — and that is especially true for minority children in urban and rural districts."

In Price's view, charter schools pose no threat to the public school system and may even strengthen that system. "Some people worry that charters will undermine schools as we know them, but an awful lot of schools really need to be reconfigured," he says.

Not surprisingly, my next question to Price dealt with vouchers. Price says that he and the National Urban League are "deeply opposed to taking public resources and channeling them into private or parochial schools. We think that such action removes public dollars from public accountability and erodes society's commitment to educate all children."

Price is very clear about what he wants to have happen. He continually employs such phrases as "Achievement matters," "Spread the gospel that achievement matters," and "Celebrate young people who do the right thing." He wants black youngsters to take their report cards to their ministers for review and discussion, and he wants those youngsters to be told, "It's nice to get an A in 'kitchen math,' but now you really need to take algebra." He cites Anthony Alvarado, a former elementary district superintendent in New York City, as a model. "He mixed high standards for youngsters and high expectations for educators and serious investment in teacher professional development, and he drove the reform agenda in New York City by understanding that — in the final analysis — education is a transaction between teachers and students. By creating a sense of excitement and mission in his school district, he was able to attract educators who wanted to be there and wanted to teach those children."

Price is convinced that teacher salaries must improve in urban and rural areas and that highly focused and effective staff development programs must be mounted. He hopes that research will be done to verify the connection that experience tells him exists "between appropriate professional development and high academic outcomes," because most of the politicians and many of the school administrators he talks to "don't get it yet."

In the November 1990 *Kappan,* Hugh Price issued a warning: "Some day, frustrated corporations, worried about where their workers will come from, and exasperated parents, fed up with unresponsive school systems, just might join forces on behalf of such truly radical reform [as vouchers]. . . . Those of us who care about universal public education ought to take heed. Nothing long taken for granted remains a given these days. . . . For the enterprise [of American public education] to survive reasonably intact, the bottom line for school reform must be brighter futures for all children."

Today, Price's warning seems prescient. In the current robust economy with its low unemployment rates, employers are clamoring for qualified workers, especially young people who have a strong background in math, experience with computers, and a strong work ethic. Meanwhile, parents across the country — not just in urban centers — are expressing concern about the quality of their local schools. Today, all Americans are being pushed to answer Hugh Price's question, "Are we putting each youngster into an educational environment that gives him or her maximum chance for success?"

Carol Gilligan

Carol Gilligan was the most literary, perhaps even poetic, of the people I interviewed. In an unhesitating voice, she spoke feelingly and accurately about her subject. It felt more like interviewing a writer, even a poet, than a psychologist. Time and again, she used paraphrase and quotation from Virginia Woolf or Shakespeare or Chekhov to clarify a point or deepen an issue.

Gilligan was also the most protective of her time of any interviewee I've met — to the point of stinginess. She did nothing obvious that I could see to prepare for the interview, other than depend on her considerable memory, intelligence, and artistic speaking ability to carry her through. Most of the interviews I've done lasted for at least 90 minutes, and some took as long as three hours. Carol Gilligan's interview ended at 53 minutes when she precipitously announced that she was going to lunch with a colleague. In the end, between information in Gilligan's books or the public domain and some additional information Carol Gilligan furnished through the mail after several follow-up phone calls, I was able to complete the article on her interesting career and important work.

Carol Gilligan is a professor in the Graduate School of Education at Harvard University, the first holder of the Patricia Albjerg Graham Chair in Gender Studies at Harvard, and the author or co-author of four books and dozens of scholarly and popular articles. She is best known for her landmark book, *In a Different Voice*, published in 1982 and still in print after selling nearly 600,000 copies in 12 languages. This book established that girls and women often approach moral decisions in a way that is different from what male researchers had identified as the "norm."

Originally published as "Restoring Lost Voices: An Interview with Carol Gilligan" in *Phi Delta Kappan* (May 2000). Used with permission.

It also established Gilligan's reputation, among both academics and the informed general public, as a significant researcher, feminist thinker, and psychologist.

In 1974, 10 years after Carol Gilligan received her Ph.D. in psychology from Harvard, she was the mother of three young boys and the wife of a psychiatrist. She did not have, and wasn't certain she would have, a full-time academic career. She had taught courses at the University of Chicago and Harvard, had been a principal investigator in a couple of research studies, had published several articles, and had even done some research and teaching with Lawrence Kohlberg and Erik Erikson at Harvard. But she was not in a regular faculty position that would lead to a permanent appointment.

In fact, Gilligan spent a great deal of time in the late Sixties and early Seventies as a social activist. At the University of Chicago, where she taught a course while her husband completed his medical internship, she was "one of the faculty members who refused to submit grades because they were being used as a basis for the Vietnam draft." She participated in sit-ins and became "active in voter registration, the civil rights movement, the anti-nuclear movement, and the women's strike for peace." The important issue of how people make moral decisions harked back to Gilligan's doctoral work and continued to percolate in her daily life and thinking, but the subject was far from the center of any academic work that she was doing.

As an undergraduate at Swarthmore College in the middle and late 1950s, Gilligan had majored in English and was comfortable in small coed classes where her views were respected and where she studied great writers who rendered male and female voices with considerable accuracy and sensitivity. However, as a graduate student at Harvard, she studied psychology in the time-honored and unquestioned patriarchal tradition, focusing on male psychologists whose work was based largely on male subjects. She "felt a dissonance in the way my professors spoke about human experience. It seemed flat to me and off. My background was literature, where the human experience was more alive in its complexity and truth." Gilligan understood that the graduate psychology lectures and conversations were different from what she had learned reading Shakespeare, Virginia Woolf, and Chekhov, but she could not yet identify the beating heart of the problem.

When Gilligan returned to Cambridge with her family in the late 1960s, she was drawn to people like Erikson and Kohlberg because of their serious interest in the intersection of psychology with political choice, literature, and philosophy. Like Gilligan, both men were committed to the civil rights and antiwar movements. In 1970, at the height of the Vietnam War, Carol Gilligan taught a section of Kohlberg's course titled Moral and Political Choice. Not long after, Gilligan began a study of Harvard students facing the Vietnam draft. She wanted to know how these young men would "act at that dramatic moment in their lives when they had to make a choice" about serving in a war many of them felt was neither legitimate nor moral.

President Nixon ended the draft in 1973, and that abruptly ended Gilligan's study; but also in 1973 the Supreme Court ruled in *Roe* v. *Wade* that state anti-abortion legislation was not legal. Gilligan immediately "picked up my study with the moment when women have to make that decision. *Roe* v. *Wade* gives women the decisive voice in a real moment of choice with real consequences for their personal lives and for society."

Everything began to converge for Gilligan between 1973 and 1977. The voices of women that she often heard in literature but failed to hear in the canon of graduate school psychology began to come through. Gilligan had been taught to consult the work of Freud, Weber, Piaget, Kohlberg, and Erikson as the touchstones against which to judge psychological health and normative experience. The work of these men — all brilliant, dedicated, and even fair-minded — was rooted almost entirely in studying white male behavior and experience. As Gilligan interviewed more and more pregnant women, a different pattern began to emerge. "I'm hearing something from women for the first time. It became, 'If I bring my voice into my relationships, will I become a bad, selfish woman, and will I end my relationships?' "

Women historically had been unable or unwilling to express what they felt. When they emphasized relationships and care over logic and justice, they were thought to be morally inferior, and they feared that they would lose their important relationships. An unmarried pregnant woman considering abortion might feel that she very much wanted the baby but that having it would cost her a relationship with a man she loved very much. Women's important moral decisions were typically based not on their own deepest feelings but on the highly respected rules of the patriarchal culture that enveloped them.

At her kitchen table, Gilligan began to write an article on what she had learned about women's conceptions of self and morality. "Suddenly a new landscape began to form around women's relationships with themselves and the world they lived in. The key issue is one of absence versus presence, and morality for women had been aligned with absence, with being selfless." If women took their cues from the dominant culture when making decisions about raising children, casting a vote, or even dealing with their own sexuality and pleasure, how could they be responsible for what they "decided" and how could they feel mature? "It all crystallized, and now I knew why I didn't feel present in graduate school, in psychology."

Gilligan submitted her piece on women's voice and the abortion decision to the *Harvard Educational Review*, which initially rejected it. But after Gilligan agreed to some compromises over the organization and style, the journal finally published the article in 1977 under the title "In a Different Voice: Women's Conception of Self and Morality." This publication rapidly catapulted Gilligan "from an on-the-edge perch to 'Who are you?' and lots of inquiries from psychologists." The article became a citation classic and was followed in 1979 by "Woman's Place in Man's Life Cycle," also published in the *Harvard Educational Review*. Both articles in revised form would become important chapters of *In a Different Voice*.

Gilligan now understood that the "arc of developmental theory" she had learned in graduate school did not include what she was learning from women and that "the problem might be with the theory — and that starts my work." She also concluded that part-time teaching, raising children, political activism, the arts, and tending an organic garden would not be enough for her. Her ideas were controversial and not yet completely developed. She needed to find a comfortable institution "that would allow me to find myself in work, give merit to my life, allow me to write about what I was learning, and eventually grant me tenure." That institution was Harvard, where, indeed, she was granted tenure in 1986.

In a Different Voice is grounded in three thoughtful studies that required close listening. The first study was of college students who had dropped out of a course on moral and political choice. Of the 20 students who had dropped the course, 16 were women. The second study focused on the abortion decisions of 29 women ranging in age from 15 to 33 and representing a variety of ethnic and social backgrounds. The third study was the rights and responsibilities study, in which a group of males and females were interviewed across the life cycle, ages 6 to 60.

Often in the book, Gilligan, the undergraduate literature major and lifelong reader of classic literature, balances the voice of Freud or Piaget with that of Chekhov or Shakespeare. She contrasts the differing views of men and women in *The Cherry Orchard* and *The Merchant of Venice* to make her points regarding the relationship between power, voice, and gender. It is Portia in *The Merchant of Venice*, played by a young male in Shakespeare's time, dressed as a female when in character but dressed as a male judge in the resolution scene, who brings the plea for mercy ("The quality of mercy is not strained") into the male citadel of justice. It is this female solution that allows resolution without hurt. In another case, a blended male/female solution or a male view might properly predominate. In this case, a woman must use a male voice to deliver a female resolution that males will find acceptable.

Without question, *In a Different Voice* was revolutionary and struck a powerful chord in both men and women. Men began to see the limits of using only male samples for studies and only male thinking as the basis for moral decisions. Scholars wanted to know, "Is this true? What's your sample? How do you know this?" Men and women sought Gilligan out to say, "You saved my marriage" or just to tell her that the book rang true with them. The responses came from the clerk in the Cambridge supermarket and the cousin of Gilligan's typist as well as from students and many academic colleagues. "I got very strong signs that I was in touch with something real; this was not rocks in Siberia."

From the time she was a child, Gilligan was always around issues far more real than rocks in Siberia. "I was a child during the Holocaust. My parents were very involved with refugees from Europe." Gilligan's preschool and high school experiences were in New York City's progressive Walden School, where moral decisions were emphasized and discussed. Her father, William Friedman, the child of Hungarian immigrants, became a very successful lawyer and took "lawyers fleeing Hitler into his law firm." Gilligan's mother, Mabel Caminez Friedman, the daughter of Ukrainian and German immigrants, "was very involved in helping refugees get settled in New York." In fact, *In a Different Voice* was dedicated to Gilligan's parents, people she referred to several times in our interview as important moral influences on her. Studying moral issues and decisions strongly appealed to Gilligan. In her preface to the 1993 edition of *In a Different Voice*, Gilligan makes the point that, after the Middle Passage and the Holocaust, social scientists cannot adopt a position of neutrality on moral issues.

Indeed, Gilligan's next work was to continue and deepen her study of female thinking and moral decisions, this time concentrating on adolescent girls. In the 1980 *Handbook of Adolescent Psychology*, edited by Joseph Edelson, there was "not enough material for a chapter on girls." Over the next several years, 1983 to 1992, Carol Gilligan and her students set out to repair the omission of girls' voices in the literature of adolescence. Gilligan began her research in the Emma Willard School, an all-girls' school in Troy, New York, with strong support and funding from the Geraldine Rockefeller Dodge Foundation. This work resulted in the 1990 book *Making Connections: The Relational Worlds of Adolescent Girls at Emma Willard School*. Her research continued in Boys' and Girls' Clubs in three ethnically different Boston neighborhoods as well as at independent and public schools in the Boston area. In the middle 1980s, Gilligan did a five-year longitudinal study of girls aged 6 through 16 at the Laurel School in Shaker Heights, Ohio. In 1992, *Meeting at the Crossroads*, based on work at the Laurel School, appeared and was selected as one of the *New York Times'* notable books of the year.

What Gilligan and her colleagues did during those years was "to revisit the psychology of adolescence, but this time listening carefully to girls without putting the interpretive frame on them that had been derived from boys." She discovered that something happened to girls between the ages of 11 and 15 or 16. During this time, it often became "dangerous" for a girl to know or say what she actually felt. The younger girls were remarkably honest and confident and courageously outspoken. Just two or three years later, they become ambiguous and timid in their answers, covering up what they knew. "This was marked in the interviews by the phrase 'I don't know.' If you stayed with them, gently probing and leaving room for answers, you found out that they did know."

When girls are initiated into the adult world, they find that most of the values are rooted in the experience of successful men. It is a world that attaches great value to independence, separation, and autonomy and not a lot of value to relationships and connection. Often, when girls struggled for connection, they were seen as too immature to achieve separation. "Girls' resilience in elementary school is suddenly at risk; you have learning problems, eating disorders, depression." An example that Gilligan gives in "Woman's Place in Man's Life Cycle" explains this. Boys play competitive games with lots of rules. They quarrel a great deal, but they enjoy the disputes and solve them. When girls get into disputes in games, they tend to end the game. "Girls are more tolerant in their attitudes toward rules, more willing to make exceptions. Girls subordinated the continuation of the game to the continuation of the relationships." Of course, in the competitive business world, it is often the boys' rules that dominate, but that is changing in a world "where women can be astronauts and men can be caregivers."

Gilligan's questions now are, What is going on with boys, and how can what she has learned about girls bring about change? With Judy Chu, a doctoral student at Harvard, she is studying boys aged four to six. "Boys are initiated into a patriarchal order at this time, and you can see it in my data on five-year-olds as they begin to cover up what they feel, to shield themselves and begin to take on a protective role." Fathers enjoy the openness of their sons until about age five, when they begin to help them "narrow their voices and become 'men' in the world, fearing that, if they remain open and vulnerable, they will be teased or bullied or shamed." Gilligan is convinced that both boys and girls must be encouraged to develop their natural voices if they are to mature into adults who can help "eradicate such crimes as violence and genocide," which blighted the 20th century.

When I asked Gilligan about the role of schools in all of this, her immediate response was that we must "amplify the voices of children." She emphasized that this is not a simple Rousseauean approach, whereby we just tell children to speak freely. Rather, we must provide extremely engaging curriculum, train teachers, and then "talk to the children, create a resonant space, and help them understand what they are saying and seeing," as she did in her work primarily with girls in Boston and other places. The teachers need to be given staff development opportunities to hear their own voices on subjects of great importance and to revisit those times when their voices were muffled. In Gilligan's experience working with schools, when the teachers felt that their work and subject matter were important and that both they and their students were expressing themselves authentically and thoughtfully, "there was a decline among the teachers of headaches and depression." When the teachers began to express themselves more honestly, the structure of the school began to change.

As Gilligan completes her new work with boys, she sees the outline of a careful "developmental map, one that will help save a huge amount of money by doing preventive work" just at those times in children's lives — ages four to six for boys and early adolescence for girls — when intervention is the most crucial and effective. Gilligan is optimistic about what schools can do but does not underestimate the difficulty. "Good schools succeed in a variety of ways, but at the core are real relationships between adults and children. We've just ended the most violent century in human history, and we know things we didn't know before about the need to live with one another. This is an incredible opportunity for the education system. It's a daunting challenge, but it's also exhilarating. It's what good teaching is all about."

John I. Goodlad

In late 1999, I spent a few hours with John Goodlad at his In-
stitute for Educational Inquiry in Seattle. Casually dressed, Pro-
fessor Goodlad, now 80, looked like a healthy, alert, successful,
65-year-old academic. We sat in a sun-filled room (sunny for only
a short time until the clouds moved in, as they so often do in
Seattle) overlooking Lake Union and the Aurora Bridge and
spoke about the last fifty years in education.

Goodlad, of course, knew all the major reform and renewal
topics; all the efforts to bring technology into education from
radio to television to computers; all the local, state, university,
and federal initiatives that had achieved some notoriety, and sev-
eral that actually had made some headway.

After all that time and effort, Goodlad's first conclusion was
that the majority of the nation's schools are doing a creditable
job. However, schools, particularly urban schools, that are filled
with poor and minority students need a great deal of help and
money. Renewal, not reform, is the way to improve schools be-
cause we usually cannot start over with a new building, faculty,
and program. Finally, the politicians and business leaders have
learned precious little from history. Seventy-four years ago, when
Goodlad began his own schooling in Canada, there was a call for
standards and tests. That call has failed again and again to help
most students, yet we are doing it again and paying little atten-
tion to the real issues of poverty, racism, serious curriculum
renewal, staff development, building a serious agenda for each
school, and other issues that would make a difference.

John Goodlad recently celebrated his 80th birthday. While he
remains extremely active both as the co-director of the University

---

Originally published as "Leadership for Change: An Interview with
John Goodlad" in *Phi Delta Kappa* (September 2000). Used with permission.

of Washington's Center for Educational Renewal and as the president of the Institute for Educational Inquiry (IEI), Goodlad is also at a point in his long and distinguished career where great honors are coming to him.

A book has been published to pay homage to Professor Goodlad and to summarize his accomplishments: *The Beat of a Different Drummer: Essays on Educational Renewal in Honor of John Goodlad* (Peter Lang Publishing, 1999). On 30 November 1999, a full-page announcement appeared in the *New York Times* proclaiming that John I. Goodlad was one of this year's recipients of the Harold W. McGraw Jr. Prize in Education. This prestigious award and a $25,000 gift are presented annually to three "outstanding individuals who have dedicated themselves to improving education in this country and whose accomplishments are making a difference today." Professor Goodlad was honored for six decades of work in education renewal, school partnerships, curriculum improvement, and the lifting of standards in education. Past recipients have included the late Ernest Boyer, Barbara Bush, and U.S. Secretary of Education Richard Riley.

I interviewed John Goodlad in Seattle at his Institute for Educational Inquiry office, a converted private home overlooking Lake Union and the Aurora Bridge. Casually dressed and looking very fit, Goodlad was full of contrarian ideas, mature judgments, and observations filtered through the lens of 60 years of experience doing everything from teaching in a one-room schoolhouse in rural Canada to serving as the dean of the Graduate School of Education at UCLA, from consulting on education in China to publishing more than 30 books as author, co-author, or editor.

When I asked Goodlad to look back over the years and tell me the first large thought that came to mind, he said without hesitation, "Over more than 60 years, the problems remain essentially the same, and the solutions remain essentially the same. If kids don't pass some arbitrary standard of what a grade means, you punish them twice. They've already experienced failure, an enormously debilitating experience, and then you tell them they have to do it all over again." From Seattle to New York, there are problems with students not showing up for mandated summer school and failing the same tests a second time and with parents complaining about interference with the needs of families.

A much more intelligent and effective way to look at problems children are having in school would be to see "youngsters' failure as a signal for help, rather than a signal for punishment." Why is the child failing? What is the school trying to do? How can the school build an agenda that the staff can get behind to tell the story of that school's mission and to provide meaningful help to every student? What sort of training do teachers and administrators need to renew the school and make it effective? What resources will the school need to be successful? These are some of the questions a school staff should be encouraged to ask. Simply telling youngsters they must pass an arbitrary test without thoughtful preparation in the school will result in little difference. "Our test scores will go up a bit, but they will not go up significantly, and they will not solve the problems of disadvantaged youngsters who arrive at school seriously handicapped — more handicapped than ever before."

School "reform" is a significant part of the school problem in Goodlad's opinion. In fact, the majority of schools in this country are doing many things very well. Most youngsters are thriving — even to the point of doing well on a range of tests, from reasonably intelligent instruments to benighted measures of little value. Educators "should stop talking about reform because it's a nasty concept that suggests bad people and bad conditions that must be reformed in somebody else's image. Renewal is much more elevating of the human spirit." Renewal is also more realistic. We are not going to knock down most buildings or dismiss whole faculties, nor should we in most places. We can renew schools by asking and answering the questions raised above. Finally, reform just doesn't work. "No model of reform recommended by serious reformers has ever made it to the showroom floor." By the time the school staff, the local authorities, the teacher associations, the politicians, and all the forces behind assessment get through with it, a reform plan is only a pale shadow of its original form.

Since the late 1930s, John Goodlad has had personal experience with virtually every issue about which he has written. Goodlad had a hardscrabble childhood, albeit a happy one, growing up in a rural Canadian town 2,500 feet up the side of a mountain overlooking Vancouver. It never occurred to him to go to college; no one in his family or immediate community had ever done so. But he managed to finish high school; and in the late 1930s, with Canada and much of the world in the vicious grip of the Great Depression, students could matriculate for a fifth year in high school (the equivalent of the first year of college) plus complete one year of normal school to qualify for a provisional teaching certificate. Over the next eight years, Goodlad taught in a one-room, eight-grade school; became principal of a small Canadian school; was appointed the director of education of the Provincial Industrial School for Boys, many labeled incorrigible delinquents; took evening and summer courses to get his bachelor's and master's degrees; got married; moved to the United States; earned a Ph.D. at the University of Chicago; and began his extraordinary career in teacher education and school renewal.

In Canada, Goodlad taught 34 children scattered across eight grades in one room — a job that initially required him to plan 56 small lessons each day. He learned to work within the system, but he also devised innovative ways to integrate subject matter and grades. Then, working with delinquent boys, Goodlad came to understand "the power of the environment to shape young people." This work in Canada was the genesis of the ideas later spelled out in detail in such books as *The Elementary School* (1956) and *The Nongraded Elementary School* (1959). *A Place Called School*, arguably Goodlad's best-known book, was published in 1984 and received the first Distinguished Book-of-the-Year Award from Kappa Delta Pi as well as the American Educational Research Association's 1985 Outstanding Book Award. It, too, owes much to the daily life Goodlad experienced as a teacher and administrator in Canadian schools. John Goodlad has consistently respected the quotidian life of schools and the hourly issues that face thoughtful teachers.

Twenty-five years in the Graduate School of Education at UCLA — as a professor, as director of the lab school, and as dean from 1967 to 1983 — brought Goodlad into very close contact with all the issues in school renewal and teacher education. That close contact with the world of schools was preceded by work at Agnes Scott College, Emory University, and the University of Chicago and continues at the University of Washington. Goodlad grew used to seeing complex education improvement plans somewhat altered by political needs; but much to his dismay, he notes that school improvement today has largely passed out of the hands of educators. "Increasingly and with declining impact, the fate of our schools is in the hands of politicians, and politicians hate to hear that problems in education are very complicated," he points out. Essentially, the politicians have embraced the behaviorist, linear model and attitudes of the corporate world. It is the corporate world that supports political campaigns, and it is Louis Gerstner Jr., the CEO of IBM, who convenes the nation's most widely publicized education meeting, not the dean of some school of education or some state commissioner of education.

Rarely do the major figures in education reform get invited to these meetings — not Theodore Sizer or James Comer or John Goodlad. Governors and corporate leaders dominate the IBM group, a few leaders of conventional education organizations get invited, President Clinton speaks, and the conferees reach consensus on many of the problems in education. The upshot of all of this, of course, is more blame placed at the doorstep of educators — including teacher educators.

Goodlad sees ironies here. First, most of the education of teachers occurs not in schools of education, but in the schools of arts and sciences. While there is a "face validity to the claim by politicians and business leaders that teachers should know their subjects," they are looking in the wrong place for the teaching. The general liberal studies departments frequently offer courses as a result of pressure from the medical, law, engineering, and business schools but rarely as a result of pressure from the schools of education. Yet, of all the divisions in a university, it is the school of education that relies most heavily on the course offerings in the arts and sciences. It is not the physicians or the business executives who make direct use of these courses as tools in their professions; it is the teachers.

Second, many schools of education have made a serious effort in the past 15 years to make their teacher training more realistic and rigorous. Politicians frequently say that more decisions should be made in the schools, and the administration and faculty should be held accountable for student achievement. At the same time, "the state and federal bureaucracies have put more and more restraints on teachers to the point of saying, in effect, teachers are not professionals. They just need a college degree, and we'll set all of the ground rules for them. It is a defensible hypothesis that today's teachers are getting much better training at many colleges and universities, but they are also far more restrained by the heavy bureaucracy when they get into the classroom." Teachers today have to spend most of their time and energy training students to take tests and teaching to those tests. Given that situation, they can pay little attention to methods and subject matter that may be far more important than what is in those paper-and-pencil tests. Limiting the power and flexibility of the teacher also makes the profession uninviting to the best and brightest students who either do not enter the profession or give up after a few years.

There is no single or simple answer to what should be done, but one important effort Goodlad thinks should be made is to educate business leaders. He understands the limits on their time, but he would like serious educators around the country to gather small groups of corporate leaders for a series of, say, three weekends over the course of a year. "The business leaders would come in with an incredible array of prejudices," but these are bright people who are used to looking at issues and problems. Most large companies have an education section; but these are not always staffed by the best educators, and they may not be giving their employers, other educators, or the general public the most sophisticated or informed advice. In fact, the people in the education section often do not even have direct access to the corporate leaders.

Goodlad is "sick and tired of being insulted by the business community's representatives." He was recently invited to a meeting sponsored by a major American corporation. The corporation's education representative talked about using ground-breaking technology in the schools and illustrated her point by showing a videotape that was little more than talking heads. Her speech was superficial and unfocused, and she referred to poorly prepared students as "dumbheads" in which her company had no interest. The educators in the audience tried to be courteous and "searched hard to find a pony in the manure pile; but frankly, if we had made a similar presentation to the business community, they would have walked out on us."

What Goodlad believes needs to be done is to gather the leaders themselves and convince them that "the workplace will not survive unless we educate people for democracy and get students to understand some of the restraints required by our own surround. Kids need to know who they are and what sort of society they are growing up in. There needs to be a profound rethinking of what 21st century democracy requires of the schools." Together, educators and business leaders need to understand to what extent schools should train students to think, to be citizens in a democracy, to command information and technology, and to have rich lives. "What we need is good direct communication between able educators and corporate leaders to see if we can arrive at some agreements about the mission of our schools and how to achieve this mission."

The bottom line in business is very important, but it should not be the only public interest of corporate America. Helping students in schools to function in the American business system is surely a concern, but it is not the *primary* aim of education. Goodlad is optimistic enough to believe that business leaders who give the time, do some serious reading, and become exposed to both the small and large issues of schooling will participate in the creation of a new narrative of what the school's mission ought to be. Issues such as the physical and psychological safety of students in schools, the development of a rich sense of self that includes important connections between the school and parents, and the matter of how to educate students to make sense of the 21st century should be discussed.

In the end, the individual schools will be led, for better or worse, by school leaders, and leadership is John Goodlad's signature. "One of the major reasons why schools don't change much is that change needs leadership. It needs committed, intelligent leadership, an agenda, an awareness of the conditions that have to be put in place, a grasp of the strategies that one has to use to effect change." As Goodlad sees it, there are two major problems here.

First, much of the education leadership training in schools of education does not give educators command of the change process. Leadership training programs, Goodlad believes, should be a "logical continuation of the best training available to be a teacher." Too much of the education leadership training is for technical management. For instance, many graduate schools of education include serious training in budgeting as part of the coursework. The fact is that most school budgets are handled by a business manager and contain very little in discretionary funds available to principals — or even superintendents. Most of a school's budget goes for salaries, fringe benefits, curriculum materials, and such fixed expenses as water, heat, and telephones. The principal might have discretionary control over $75,000. He or she needs to be honest and mature, but not an expert at budgeting. Much like teaching, school leadership is essentially about working with people and improving instruction. Most schools in this country have fewer than 1,000 students. "Schooling is largely a local cottage industry that involves people, and it is people skills that are needed."

The second issue is that change requires leadership over a long period of time, and most school leaders "don't stay in the job long enough to effect change." From college presidents to assistant principals, there is a constant effort to move to a more prestigious job or a job at a "higher" level. Continuity in leadership is the central problem. In one doctoral study at the University of Washington, the data showed that, as soon as respected teachers showed clear signs of leadership in their schools, they were assigned part of the time to special tasks in the central office. The most successful districts connected to the National Network for Educational Renewal (NNER) have found ways to increase leadership capacity to the point where two or three changes in leadership positions make little difference in a school or system, for there are many leaders and a large number of staff members who believe in the renewal effort.

Leadership training must have two emphases. First, prospective leaders must be trained in methods that really apply in schools, such as building an agenda for renewal and getting colleagues to help pursue that agenda. Leadership programs should focus on the principalship because most school leadership and change occur at the building level. Second, Goodlad argues, "if you are going to engage in a significant process of renewal, there must be a continuing critical mass of people who are committed to the agenda, who are willing to spend the time, and who get rewarded for spending the time." Training and achieving critical mass are related. Training takes place over time, perhaps two or three years, and must be thoughtful and informed. It involves a great deal of reading, meeting with leaders and prospective leaders, observing places that have had success, and learning how to build a clear agenda for renewal. At the same time, it is crucial to build a critical mass of support in a school or school district. It does little good to have one or two people committed to a renewal plan that will surely languish when they leave.

It is not possible to talk about schooling in America in 2000 and beyond without some comment on such front-burner issues as charter schools, vouchers, and poverty. Goodlad believes that "every school should be a charter school in the sense of being able to write a charter about what it is for and what it ought to be able to do." Essentially, a school charter is the equivalent of what Goodlad means when he talks about building an agenda. Every school should be able to say what its mission is, what sort of renewal it wishes to undertake, and what resources, training, and strategies will be needed for the school to be successful.

Goodlad has an unusual take on the concept of vouchers. He would allow youngsters, particularly those in small schools, to use up to 10% of the cost of their education in that district for special training that is not available in the school. For instance, if a child were talented in music or dance and could not be accommodated in the school, the family might receive a voucher for private violin or modern dance lessons. This would fulfill "our commitment to develop the individual talents of youngsters and to provide a diverse curriculum for children." Goodlad sees the use of vouchers to attend a private school as destructive. "Vouchers that permit a child to go to a school perceived to be good destroy the notion that all our schools must be commonly good." Too many parents would select the allegedly good school solely on the basis of test scores "because that's the criterion we're using." And test scores may not be the only — or even the best — measure that should be considered. In addition, vouchers would defeat the idea of public education and play into the hands of people who want to privatize schools and make a profit from schooling. To be sure, public schools need strong missions, well-prepared leaders, and excellent teachers — all conditions we should work toward. Public schools also need "more freedom to set and follow their own course" without constant interference from bureaucracies.

Ten years ago, during the 1988-1991 recession, many of the leaders I interviewed were focused on improving schooling in poor areas as a way to help disadvantaged youngsters out of the cycle of inadequate education and no jobs or dead-end jobs. That has changed. Today, such people as Jesse Jackson, Harold Howe II, and James Comer believe that the fundamental problem may be economic. John Goodlad is in agreement with this. "If we want to improve schooling in the United States, the wealthiest country in the world must address poverty. The most direct way of improving achievement in schools is to improve the financial resources of the family." Fifty years of research tells us that the better off families are financially, the better the education their children get both at home and in school.

Goodlad is particularly concerned about the number of times per year poor children move, since mobility has a "highly negative impact on school performance." Some children in cities are moved to three or four schools in a single year as a result of financial contingencies or placements in foster homes. Improving schooling remains a laudable and worthwhile goal, but getting at the conditions of poverty is critical. Although we have no shortage of ideas about how to improve schooling in poor areas, "we may be reaching the limit of how much improvement we can make in these schools without addressing the issues of poverty and mobility directly."

The public perception of education worries Goodlad, and he feels that part of the problem may be manufactured, rather than real. "Where does all the dissatisfaction come from? The research on this is sloppy." Is the dissatisfaction with the schools, or is it dissatisfaction with the uninvited changes imposed on the schools by requiring more and more paper-and-pencil tests that often do not measure good education? The polling research is fairly consistent in that "the local school gets a pretty good rating, but schooling in general gets a lower rating." This suggests a widespread view that "the school in my immediate community is fairly good, but I keep reading and hearing that the schools are terrible. How can most local schools be good and, simultaneously, most schools in the nation be bad?"

John Goodlad's work in education renewal continues through the University of Washington's Center for Educational Renewal and the Institute for Educational Inquiry. About 1,200 people have gone through either the IEI's leadership program or a local version through one of the NNER settings. About 140 people around the country have been so thoroughly prepared that they are qualified to lead similar programs. What Goodlad presses for in a consistent and optimistic way is a time "when the education community gives affirmation that we're doing many things well and that there are several large-minded issues we can agree upon

— and not be subject to the constant pushes in different directions from politicians and business leaders and not have to constantly defend ourselves against the accusation that we're not doing anything well."

About the Author

Dr. Goldberg retired as a public school administrator in 1994 and is now an education writer, book editor, and consultant. He has written more than 80 articles on educational and social issues. His previous book is titled *How to Design an Advisory System for a Secondary School* (ASCD, 1998). Goldberg currently is working on a handbook on education leadership. Mark Goldberg can be reached at Mark12738@aol.com.